The Passages We Celebrate

Commentary on the Scripture Texts for Baptisms, Weddings and Funerals

Patricia Datchuck Sánchez

Sheed & Ward

Sheed & Ward™ is a service of The National Catholic Reporter Publishing Company.

Library of Congress Cataloguing-in-Publication Data
Sánchez, Patricia Datchuck.
    The passages we celebrate : commentary on the Scripture texts for baptisms, weddings and funerals / Patricia Datchuck Sánchez.
        p.   cm.
    ISBN 1-55612-663-8
    1. Baptism—Biblical teaching. 2. Marriage—Biblical teaching. 3. Death—Biblical teaching. 4. Catholic Church—Liturgy.
    I. Title.
BX2210.S26   1994
251—dc20   94-30523
                                                          CIP

Published by: Sheed & Ward
                   115 E. Armour Blvd.
                   P.O. Box 419492
                   Kansas City, MO 64141

To order, call: (800) 333-7373

Contents

Part III
Readings for Funerals

Second Reading

Gospel

Dedication

For Rafael,
without whom none of this would have been possible and with
whom it has been a labor of love . . .

and for Paul, Rafael, Madalena and Patrick,
with a hope that they will always know both the challenge and
the comfort of the Word, as they experience the passages in
their lives.

Prologue

*I*n the course of every human life there are a series of transitions which mark the stages of growth and development of the human person. At times these transitions are easily discernible, because of the struggles by which they have become characterized, e.g. the terrible twos, the turbulent teens, the mid-life crises, etc. At other times, the changes are subtle, nuanced by experience and wisdom.

As each of us struggles with these transitions, we also learn to understand, to accept, and to become who we are; we engage in that process which experts in human development have variously referred to as individuation, self-actualization, autonomy and/or integration.

For those among us who are believers, these processes of growth and transition are inextricably bound to our faith in the person and mission of Jesus Christ. Because of this faith, the transitions of life may be thought of as *passages*.

As believers in Christ, our life in him and within the community which professes him is initiated by the watery passage of baptism. When individuals marry, they embark together on a passage which weaves two separate lives into one loving, lasting and mutual partnership. At death, each of us traverses the inexorable and final passage to fuller, freer life.

This book was written to help those who minister to others and who share with them the experiences of life's many passages. The commentary on each of the biblical selections for baptisms, weddings, and funerals was inspired by the fact that the passages of life are graced moments to be celebrated together in faith, hope and love.

Once again, I extend to William Freburger, editor of *Celebration,* my admiration and gratitude for his continued help and encouragement in my work.

PART I

READINGS FOR BAPTISMS

First Reading

EXODUS 17:3-7

Is the Lord in our midst or not?

Visitors to the subterranean catacomb of St. Callistus in Rome experience the rich spiritual legacy of Christianity, dating from as early as the second century CE. Thousands of paintings, inscriptions and symbols attest to the faith of an often persecuted yet vibrant community of believers. In both the Crypt of the Sheep and the Crypt of the Sacraments (named for the artwork they contain), ancient artists have rendered their versions of Moses bringing forth water from the rock at Rephidim. Early believers in Jesus understood this miracle of life-giving water in the desert as a type or symbol of Christian baptism.

Preserved among the most ancient of the Hebrew traditions, this short narrative from the Yahwist (J) source is part of a longer section of the book of Exodus (15:22-17:16) that summarizes Israel's desert experience. According to the narrative, no sooner had Moses and the escapees from Egypt made their watery passage from slavery to freedom than they began to question the quality of their new existence and the God who had made it a reality for them.

In a series of murmuring incidents, the people complained bitterly against Moses. First, they grumbled about the lack of pure water—and God revealed himself as their healer (Exodus 15:22-26). Then the people complained about the lack of food—and God revealed himself as their daily and constant provider (Exodus 16). Finally, the people complained at the lack of water—and, in providing for their thirst, God revealed himself as the source of their life and sustenance.

Each of the murmuring episodes is similar in structure, based on the pattern of the "rib" or legal argument. Because of the stereotypical style, scholars regard these incidents not simply as complaints about food and/or water but as a representation of Israel's long and checkered relationship with the Lord. Moreover, Israel's "gripes" about its needs and physical discomforts in the desert are symptomatic of a deeper problem, namely, a lack of faith and trust in the Lord.

At the heart of each murmuring incident (and at the crux of this narrative) is the question, "Is the Lord in our midst or not?" (v. 7). To ask this question is to stand on the threshold of belief. Each time the people of Israel questioned the presence, the care and/or the power of the Lord, they received their answer in the form of a challenge: Would they believe in the one who ceaselessly revealed himself as their ever-present and powerful creator and caretaker?

Like ancient Israel who was freed from slavery by the passage through the Sea of Reeds and who was invited to become the very people of God, those who are baptized experience a similar passage. Through this sacrament of initiation, those baptized with water pass from slavery to sin and death and are incorporated into the life of Jesus and the church. The baptized are empowered by the Spirit and are privileged to share in the relationship of Jesus with the Father. Thus graced and strengthened, the baptized are equipped to meet those challenges in life that could result in grumbling. In faith, they can confront the question, "Is the Lord in our midst or not?"

New heart, new spirit

Rituals of purification formed an integral aspect of ancient Hebrew religion. Purity or cleanness was regarded as freedom from all physical, ritual and/or ethical defilement. Those who strove to maintain such purity were motivated by the command, "You shall be holy for I the Lord your God am holy" (Leviticus 19:2).

Over the centuries, a vast compendium of laws gradually accrued, and legislation anticipated every condition of uncleanness in minute detail. Uncleanness was typically overcome by rituals which included: (1) a specific period of waiting, usually spent apart from the community; (2) a cleansing with water; and (3) a sacrificial offering. The cleansing with water (ritual ablution) at the heart of this text from Ezekiel was understood as an external sign of an interior disposition of spiritual holiness and purity.

Deported from Judah among the first wave of exiles in 597 BCE, Ezekiel ministered among his coreligionists in the Babylonian city of Tel Abib on the banks of the Chebar river. For over 20 years, he labored as their "watchman" (Ezekiel 3:17), warning of sin's destruction and signaling the path to a new beginning in the Lord.

Polluted by their sins of idolatry and defiled by their numerous breaches of the covenant, the people in exile stood in need of a healing which could only be accomplished by the cleansing power of divine forgiveness.

This short pericope is part of a longer section (Ezekiel 34-37) in which the prophet detailed the divine plan for recreating and reestablishing the chosen people. This text underscores the fact that true cleanness or holiness comes from within, that is, from the heart.

Ancient Hebrew thought considered the heart to be the seat of a person's intelligence, spiritual strength and passion. In the heart, intentions and plans were formed; from the heart sprang the will and impulses that caused a person to act. Israel's heart had become "stony," hardened by sin to the promptings of grace and the ways of the law.

In order to restore his people to holiness and to himself, God promised them a new heart and a new spirit. Without excluding human freedom, God's gracious gifts engaged and enlisted the best efforts of his people. In other words, Israel was offered a new beginning, a new attempt at living in harmony with the God who had called them into being. Israel was challenged to appropriate the divine gift of rebirth through the response of a sincere return to the Lord.

Christian baptism affords the believer a similar rebirth. Those sprinkled with the waters of baptism are cleansed from sin and from the exile sin imposes. They are called to live in purity of heart. Enlivened with God's own Spirit, baptized believers are daily engaged by God to begin life anew—in union with the Lord and in harmony with one another.

Water, water everywhere . . .

*T*he great saga of our salvation frequently features the element of water. Both the Hebrew and Christian scriptures are replete with illustrations and analogies based on the vivifying, terrifying and purifying properties of water. In an area of the world where water is a scarce commodity, its presence produces miraculous changes in an otherwise arid and barren environment. Water is a powerful and eloquent symbol.

In the primeval history (Genesis 1-11), water was the site of God's creative power (Genesis 1:2) and the source of his gift of fertility to the earth. Eden's garden, made lush and fruitful by the presence of four rivers (Genesis 2:10-14), remains a symbol of a paradisiacal existence. When sin corrupted humanity, the ancient author interpreted the devastating waters of the mythic flood as the purifying power of God.

Choosing a people for himself, God first led them from slavery to freedom through the waters of the Sea of Reeds. Thereafter, Israel looked to that watery passage as its moment of birth as a nation. It regarded water as a source of life and sign of divine blessing (Psalm 104). In developing its sacred rituals, Israel incorporated washing with water as a symbol of moral purity (Isaiah 1:16). Similarly, God's forgiveness of the sinner was expressed as being "washed" from guilt (Psalm 51:4).

Calling their people to be attentive to God, the prophets compared the word of God to the rainwater that transforms the desert with flowers and fruit (Isaiah 55:10-11, Amos 8:11f), and the teaching of God to life-giving water (Isaiah 55:1; Sirach 15:3, 24:25-31). Apart from God, humankind is like the parched and waterless earth (Psalm 143:6), but with God we flourish like a watered garden (Isaiah 58:11).

When the sixth century BCE prophet Ezekiel attempted to bolster the hopes of his fellow exiles in Babylon, he drew upon their shared tradition of water imagery. This pericope with its description of the water flowing from the temple is part of a longer section of Ezekiel's work (chapters 40-48) in which he shares with the people his vision of the Israel soon to be restored.

Accompanied by an angelic guide, Ezekiel leads his readers on a tour of the rebuilt city of Jerusalem which has been given a new name, "The Lord is here!" (Ezekiel 48:35). In the center of the city is the temple, made radiant by the presence or glory of God which has returned (see Ezekiel, chapters 10 and 43).

Ezekiel described the renewed presence of God among his people in terms of a great river that flows from the temple to the salt water of the Dead Sea, bringing life and healing to all in its path. For the returning exiles, it would be like the rebirth of a new exodus. Washed from sin and forgiven by God, they would return to quench their thirst on his word and find new life in his law.

When Christians celebrate the sacrament of baptism with water, we also celebrate and renew in our own lives the great wealth of meaning associated with water in our Judaeo-Christian heritage.

Second Reading

ROMANS 6:3-5

Baptism now and forever

---

*I*n the 400 years between the Reformation and Vatican II, Roman Catholics experienced relatively little change with regard to sacramental theology. Since Vatican II, however, renewed emphasis has fallen on understanding the sacraments as "signs." Underscoring the teaching of the Council of Trent (Decree on the Sacraments; session VII, 1547) as well as the writings of Thomas Aquinas (Summa Theologica III, qq. 60-65) and Augustine, post-conciliar theologians describe the sacraments as: (1) signs that proclaim faith, (2) signs that express worship, (3) signs of the church's unity, and (4) signs of Christ's presence. Although the apostle Paul did not use these specific terms, his theology of the sacraments reflects similar insights.

In his letter to the Christians in Rome, Paul laid out the good news of salvation as he had been preaching it. Within that context, he explained the significance and effects of Christian baptism. Reminding the Romans of the instructions they had received as catechumens ("Are you not aware . . ."), Paul explored with them the quality of life they had begun to enjoy by virtue of their baptism. Having established their solidarity with Adam (Romans 5:12-19) and, therefore, the influence of sin in their lives, Paul then proceeded to describe the transforming power experienced by those who are baptized *eis Christon*, into Christ Jesus and his death.

By using this very dramatic prepositional phrase, Paul underscored the fact that Christians are not merely identified with the dying Christ but are incorporated into the very process by which Christ redeemed humankind from sin and death. Writing in Greek, Paul used the prefix *syn* ("with") five times within this brief text, thus emphasizing the union of the believer and Christ.

Dead *with* Christ, buried *with* Christ, raised *with* Christ, the believer lives *with* Christ, forever united *with* him.

Because the early church commonly practiced baptism by immersion, the very rite of the sacrament was itself a sign of the spiritual formation taking place. Going down into the water, believers signified their dying with Christ to sin and death. Immersed in the water, believers signified their burial with Christ. Coming up out of the water, they signified their rising with Christ to "walk in newness of life" (Romans 6:4, literal translation).

"To walk" was a term scriptural authors (both Hebrew and Christian) frequently used to indicate a certain way or style of living. To walk in God's ways meant that one had embraced a lifestyle characterized by conscious ethical behavior. Incorporated into Christ's dying and rising, the believer is thereby empowered to walk with Christ, i.e., to make conscious and deliberate decisions for Christ, with Christ, against sin.

This pericope from Romans also reflects Paul's understanding of eschatology. While he obviously directed his hopes to a future and eternal union with Christ and the Father, his use of verbs in the present tense reveals his awareness that already here and now the believer lives life in Christ.

Some (C. H. Dodd, R. Bultmann) described this as "realized eschatology," but J. Fitzmyer prefers to style Paul's thought as an "inaugurated eschatology." As Fitzmyer explains, Paul understood that believers already live in the age of salvation inaugurated by Christ, looking back to the first Good Friday and Easter Sunday and forward to a final glorious consummation.

At baptism, the believer begins to live in the age of Christ's salvation and to participate in the process of daily dying and rising. In baptism, the believer becomes a sign of life, a sacrament of hope for the world.

God is for us

---

*B*efore his encounter with the risen Lord on the road to Damascus, Paul had been zealous in his commitment to the law. Like his fellow Jews, Paul believed he could be justified (i.e., enjoy a right and saving relationship with God) by diligent observance of the law. Through the experience of his conversion to Christ, he learned that justification and/or salvation was not a *reward* earned by the righteous but was rather the undeserved *gift* of a loving God to sinners.

Paul also understood that faith is the only appropriate response to God and that baptism is the means by which the believer enters into Christ's very life and begins to appropriate the divine blessings. In his letter to the church at Rome, Paul thoroughly explored and explained these insights into the good news.

Think of Romans 8 as a *verbal* celebration of God's gifts. Within this chapter, Paul explains that the vital principle through which and from which believers now live is the Spirit of God. By virtue of the Spirit, believers are freed from the law and the flesh and become privileged heirs of Christ, children of God who can call him Abba, i.e., Papa or Daddy. Moreover, by virtue of the Spirit of God, believers are empowered to pray rightly and to hope for the glory yet to be revealed.

This pericope comprises part of the conclusion of Romans 8. Herein Paul reminds his fellow Christians that everything they enjoy in Christ has come to them, not through their own efforts but through God's initiative. The verbs "called," "foreknew" and "predestined" may be troubling but it was not Paul's intention to imply that some are chosen and others are not. Nor was he denying the freedom humans have to listen and to respond to God, or to choose not to do so.

Like the rest of the scriptural authors, Paul made no distinction between God's active will (which intends the salvation of all peoples) and God's passive or permissive will (which respects human freedom and allows persons to choose or reject him). On the contrary, Paul regarded everything as an expression of God's active will.

With the help of contemporary theology, we can complement Paul's thoughts and better understand his intentions; he merely wished to assure his Roman readers of God's constant love and support. As John Heil has noted, Paul wanted the Romans to enjoy an "indubitable certainty" about the future, because it depended not on them but on God.

As proof of his conviction that "God is for us" and "makes all things work together for the good," Paul reminds his readers that God has already given us his Son. This supreme act of divine love should obviate any anxiety about the future. In a sense, Paul was helping his Roman readers to gain a proper perspective on life by focusing on the gift of God in Christ Jesus.

Given that central focus, all the other aspects of human life fall into place. Rather than overwhelm the believers, life's petty concerns pale into insignificance; even difficult struggles and sufferings become more readily bearable. For Paul's first century readers, his words were no doubt a comfort and a strength as they faced growing opposition and intolerance from the Roman government.

Paul's 20th-century readers are also encouraged. By virtue of our baptism into Christ, we have become beneficiaries of God's goodness and love. We have the joy of knowing that God is for us, making all things work together for our good.

One body, one Spirit

As the apostolic founder of the Christian community at Corinth, Paul was often called upon to settle disputes, answer questions and regulate the spiritual activities of the bustling metropolis. In his 18 months of working and preaching in Corinth, Paul had succeeded in establishing an enthusiastic community with which he maintained contact through messengers and letters. Because of its strategic location (Corinth controlled two harbors as well as the overland passage from the Greek mainland to the Peloponnesus), Paul hoped that the city would prove to be a central base of operations from which missionaries could bring the gospel east to Asia and west to Europe. But for all its zeal in Christ, Corinth was a community wracked by division.

Some members of the community permitted their loyalties to certain preachers to deter from church unity. Others argued for the superiority of one lifestyle over another (e.g., celibate vs. married life). Distinctive traditions with regard to food, feasts, etc., caused difficulties among believers from different cultural backgrounds. Even the exercise of spiritual gifts caused dissension, as some argued that their charisms were more important than those of others. Unfortunately, the factiousness in Corinth manifested itself in every social situation and even threatened to negate the union of the community as it celebrated its life in Christ at the eucharist.

When Paul wrote to the Christians in Corinth, his concern for their unity and mutual respect for one another is obvious. This reading represents the introduction to Paul's analogous comparison of the body with its many parts to the church and its diverse members. No doubt the Greek Christians in Corinth were familiar with the analogy of the body because it was a metaphor commonly used by the Stoic philosophers who had a school in the city. An analogy easily understood, the image of the *living* body encouraged the Corinthians to understand themselves as integral and interconnected parts of an organic whole. As such, they would more readily understand the *fatal* threat their competiveness posed to the community.

In Paul's statement, "So it is with Christ," the Christ to whom the apostle refers is the Christian community itself (see 1 Corinthians 6:15 where Paul uses "Christ" as a predicate of the church in Corinth). Through their baptism, the community of individual believers was united by one principle of vitality, namely, the Spirit. Thus empowered, the community with all its diverse members becomes the visible and tangible representation of Christ for the world.

Significantly, Paul did not criticize the Corinthians for diversity but only for their divisiveness. He challenged them to replace their competitive and factious behavior with mutual respect for one another's differences. Moreover, he encouraged them to appreciate their distinctions and to engage in a cooperative interdependence that fostered and benefited from the gifts of each community member.

The Corinthian church can be understood as a microcosm of the church today. Our global communion of believers is even more culturally and charismatically diverse than that of Paul's day. Nevertheless, his pastoral advice remains relevant. We who are "Christ" in the 20th-century world are baptized into one body, enlivened by one and the same Spirit.

In Christ

---

*P*aul's founding of the church in Galatia (Asia Minor) was a serendipitous event: An illness forced him to pause temporarily from his missionary travels and to remain among the gentiles in Galatia until his condition improved (Galatians 4:13-16). As he healed physically, Paul spent himself spiritually, preaching the good news of salvation as God's free gift extended to all peoples through the cross of Christ.

When Paul moved on from the Galatian territories, the foundations he left behind were soon threatened by certain Judaizing Christian missionaries. Their claim that Paul had preached a second-rate, law-free and diluted gospel and their attacks upon his apostolic authority wreaked havoc within the fledgling communities. Paul's reaction (as preserved in his letter to the Galatians) was swift and stern.

While the Judaizers demanded that the gentiles first embrace Moses, the law and circumcision before they could enjoy the salvation Christ had accomplished, Paul remained firm in his conviction that justification—or a right relationship with God—was accomplished, not through the works of the law but through faith in the gracious gift of God.

Defending himself against those who opposed his socalled "law-free" gospel, Paul explained that the law had indeed served a valuable purpose in that it had been the *paidagogos* ("pedagogue") for humanity. A pedagogue was a servant or slave entrusted with the care of a young boy; this custodian saw to it that the child went to school, monitored his studies and provided guidance in the form of discipline and restraint (Galatians 3:24-25).

But like the pedagogue whose services were no longer needed when the child grew to adulthood, so did the law's role come to an end with the coming of Christ. This short pericope picks up Paul's argument at this point, underscoring the fact that a saving relationship can no longer be understood in terms of what we do (i.e., the works of the law) but of who we are and have become in Christ Jesus.

By his saving death on the cross, Christ has afforded every believer the blessing of becoming a child of God. No longer relegated to the custodianship of the law (*paidagogos*), the believer enjoys the dignity and freedom of a direct relationship with the Father in Christ.

"In Christ" or "into Christ" (*en Christo*) appears over 160 times in the Pauline letters. By this expression, Paul described the mode of union or identity with Christ achieved through the baptism of the believer. As J. Fitzmyer explains, "Baptism is the sacramental complement of faith, the rite whereby a person achieves union with Christ and publicly manifests his commitment."

Paul also referred to the identification of the baptized believer with the Lord in terms of "putting on" or being "clothed with" Christ. Those of Greek descent among Paul's readers would have recognized these terms. Similar phrases were used in the mystery cults wherein the initiates clothed themselves in the apparel of the god with whom they wished to be identified. Paul's Jewish readers would have understood these terms in light of their significance in the Hebrew scriptures where to "put on" or be "clothed with" meant to take on the attitude, virtue or moral conviction of another (Psalm 132:9, Job 29:14, Isaiah 59:17).

Those who have been clothed with Christ in baptism and who share in his relationship as children of the Father are also initiated into a new mode of relationship with one another. All distinctions as to race and sex, all inequities with regard to social status pale into insignificance when compared with the union with one another that baptized believers have in Christ.

One baptism, one Lord

*I*n Paul's day, the port city of Ephesus in western Asia Minor (modern day Seljuk in Turkey) was the fourth largest city in the vast Roman empire. The impressive 24,000-seat amphitheater, unearthed in this century by Austrian archaeologists, was no doubt known to Paul who, with Priscilla and Aquila, labored for over two years to bring the good news to the Ephesians (see Acts 19).

While Paul's authorship of the letter to the Ephesians went virtually unquestioned until the late 18th century, many modern scholars now attribute the letter to a Pauline disciple writing several years after the apostle's death. Whoever wrote the letter was familiar with Paul's thought and theology, and seemed intent upon portraying Paul, in his suffering and service for the gospel's sake, as a model and inspiration for all believers. The general tone of the letter and the omission of an addressee (in Ephesians 1:1) in the earliest manuscripts suggest that the text may have been intended as a circular letter for several of the churches in Asia Minor.

A composite of doctrinal teaching and paranetic preaching, this beautiful letter centers on the unity of all things in Christ and the role of the church in sustaining that unity. This pericope represents part of the letter's paranetic portion, i.e., the persuasive preaching by which the author attempts to help his readers respond practically to the letter's doctrine.

To that end, with the letter's central theme in mind, the author challenges his readers to translate the union they experience by their baptism into Christ into every aspect of their communal life. Like Christ who came to reconcile all humanity to the Father, so must the church live to reconcile all in Christ.

To prove themselves worthy of their call to follow Christ, believers were to put into practice virtues which, by ancient worldly standards, were thought to be subservient and even ignoble. Humility, meekness, patience and forbearance were considered the way of the weak who had no other option but to eke out a servile existence in the world. Independence and self-righteousness, on the other hand, were regarded as the qualities of the strong and intelligent.

But Christ's coming into the world and the revelation in him of God's mercy and love (Ephesians 2:1-5) made humanity conscious of its sin and of the need for salvation. Therefore, the believer who has come to know the reconciling power of the cross can only respond to that great gift with the humble and gentle attitude of Christ himself.

In a catena of seven expressions of oneness, the author of Ephesians celebrates the unity of Christians with Christ and with one another. By *one baptism*, the believer becomes firmly rooted in Christ who is the *one Lord*. Enlivened by the *one Spirit* and impelled by *one hope*, believers live as *one body*, professing *one faith* in the *one God* and Father of all. Some scholars suggest that these "one formulas" were used in early baptismal liturgies as joyous shouts of praise.

The church which professes Christ has greatly evolved over the centuries and its missionary efforts have reached into every culture. Pluralism and diversity have become the norm; nevertheless, the challenge to maintain a vital unity in Christ remains the constant vocation of every believer.

God's chosen people

One of the seven "catholic" epistles or general letters not directed to a specific church, 1 Peter is a pastoral document addressed to a broad audience of gentile believers in Asia Minor. Referred to by the author as "strangers" and "sojourners in exile" (1:1, 2:11), these gentile converts to Christ had, by virtue of their baptism, become alienated from and disowned by their respective societies. Exposed to persecution (which ran the gamut from subtle prejudice to open political hostility), the recipients of 1 Peter were encouraged through this letter to keep the faith and to regard their struggles as a share in the sufferings of Christ himself (1 Peter 4:12-19).

Tradition attributes the letter to Peter, but recent scholarship suggests that 1 Peter was more likely the work of a second or third generation, Greek-speaking Christian writing pseudonymously from Rome. Intent upon helping his readers find their rootedness in Christ and to forge an identity for themselves within an unwelcoming environment, the author of 1 Peter encouraged these early converts to understand that they had been reborn as a new people of God through baptism. By virtue of their sacramental union with Christ, they had become a people defined not by race, nationality or geographical boundaries but by the very blood of Christ (1 Peter 1:18-21).

In an effort to help his readers realize their identity and responsibility as a Christian people, the author drew upon several rich and graphic metaphors from the Hebrew scriptures. Just as Israel had been a foundation stone for the people of God (Isaiah 28:16) and just as Christ had been a living stone rejected by humanity but a precious cornerstone in God's eyes (Psalm 118:22), so are those who are baptized into Christ to be living stones who, despite persecution, form a spiritual edifice, i.e., the church.

Drawing on titles that were the prerogative of ancient Israel and applying them to the church, the author identified those who ministered within the new household of God as: (1) a holy and royal priesthood, (2) a chosen race, (3) a holy nation (Exodus 19:5-6, Isaiah 43:20-21).

As priests, baptized believers are to be, for one another and for the world, *pontifices* (Latin *pontifex* = "priest"), literally "bridge builders." By being the place of encounter between God and his people, Christians by their very lives provide access to God. Like the priests of ancient Israel, Christians are also to offer sacrifice, not animal or grain offerings but the gift of themselves, their time, their talent, their treasure, united with the saving sacrifice of Jesus.

Just as God's choice of Israel made it a holy nation, so the church, the new Israel, is made holy by the baptismal call to follow Christ. "Holy" (Greek *hagios*) means "set apart" or "separate." Believers in Christ are holy not only by virtue of God's choice but also by their response to that choice.

Set apart for life in Christ, baptized believers express their holiness by conforming to the highest standard of behavior, i.e., to Christ himself.

This quality of life empowers the believer to proclaim the glorious works of God. Ancient Israel lived to proclaim the wonders God had wrought in liberating his people from slavery in Egypt. As the new Israel, the church lives to proclaim the glorious works of God whose Son died to liberate all of humanity from enslavement to sin and death.

By the daily renewal of their baptismal commitment, believers remain constant in their proclamation of God's glorious works. This daily living witness brings light to a world darkened by its need for God.

Gospel

MATTHEW 22:35-40

Love of God, love of neighbor

*M*any scholars regard the description of the scribe at the conclusion of Matthew's discourse on the parables as the evangelist's self-portrait and signature to the gospel. As a Christian scribe trained for the kingdom, Matthew labored to bring out of his storeroom both the new and the old (Matthew 13:52). Writing for a predominantly Jewish Christian audience, Matthew struggled to help his contemporaries appreciate Jesus as their long-expected messiah, but also as the one who would bring *new* meaning and a *new* universal purpose to Israel's expectations. As such, we see the Jesus of Matthew's gospel embracing and affirming the traditions of his people, yet all the while "pushing the envelope" of those traditions to bring them to a previously unexpected fulfillment. To that end, the evangelist repeatedly portrays Jesus in conflict with the accepted authorities of his day. This pericope represents one in a series of four controversies in which Jesus clashes with the official Jewish magisterium. In this case, the dispute hinges upon the greatest law or, more correctly, the linchpin upon which the rest of the law depends and in which it is essentially expressed.

In this particular instance, the controversy involves Jesus with the Pharisees and scribes. The scribes or lawyers were proud of their astuteness in knowing and interpreting the law while the Pharisees excelled in implementing even the minutest prescriptions of the law. Fond of legal discussions, these two groups were known to engage eminent rabbis in debate. Their question to Jesus was intended to entrap him and undermine his authority to teach.

Jesus' response encapsulated the law by pairing two laws already known to his contemporaries. Citing first from the *Shema' Israel*, a prayer derived from Deuteronomy 6:4-5, Jesus reminded his questioners that the love of God must be the first concern of every believer. More than a mere feeling, love in this context referred to that fidelity to the covenant relationship which entailed one's whole being, heart, soul and mind. More than a matter of willing and doing, this love of God was to be the focus and motivation in every aspect of human activity. The rabbis regarded this first law cited by Jesus as a "heavy" or very important one.

Naming a second law, Jesus drew on part of Israel's social legislation from the book of Leviticus (19:18). Loving one's neighbor as oneself required that the believer replace conceit with altruism. While Israelites considered the term "neighbor" to apply simply to fellow Israelites, Jesus' subsequent teachings made it clear that traditional concepts were to yield to a more universal concern.

Although Jesus' citation of these laws was not unique—others had quoted similar linchpins for the law—nevertheless, the fact that Jesus paired a "heavy" law (Deuteronomy 6:5) with a so-called "light" one (Leviticus 19:18) was indeed unique. By doing so, Jesus created an interdependence between love of God and love of neighbor, so that the keeping of each law expressed and ratified the other. As J. P. Meier has noted, "God must come first, but there is no true love of him which is not incarnated in love of neighbor."

Making disciples

Part of the great commission with which the Matthean gospel concludes, the mandate of the risen Lord to his disciples consists of three major aspects, each of which represents a major theme of this gospel.

In the first instance, the risen Lord proclaims that full and universal authority has been given to him. Earlier in the gospel, in a discussion of the Father's saving plan for humanity (a plan fully revealed only to the Son and then to those to whom the Son wishes to make it known), Jesus had intimated a share in divine authority (Matthew 11:27). Here at the end of the gospel, in resurrected glory, Jesus' declaration of his authority portrays him as the apocalyptic Son of Man upon whom would be conferred eternal sovereignty, glory and kingship over all the peoples of the earth (Daniel 7:14).

By embracing the Father's plan of salvation, i.e., by accepting the path to glory which led first to suffering and death on the cross, Jesus has become the highly exalted Son of Man. In ensuing years, those who would become his followers through baptism would experience a similar path through suffering to glory.

The second major aspect of the apostolic mandate is the inauguration of the church's universal mission. Notice the fact that the sending forth of the disciples flows directly from the authority Jesus has received as the resurrected Lord ("Go, therefore," v. 19). Empowered with the authority derived from the Christ-event, the eleven are sent forth to engage in a mission of making disciples by baptizing and by teaching.

"Make disciples of" (Greek *matheteusate*) is a dynamic process with which the whole of Matthew's gospel has been concerned. Discipleship entails: recognition and acceptance of Jesus and his unexpected style of messiahship, relinquishing one's status as a chosen people to embrace all others as brothers and sisters included in God's saving plan, coming to grips with the contradiction of the cross and realizing its redemptive mystery and, finally, becoming an avid believer in all that God has done in Jesus.

Baptism in the name of the Father, Son and Spirit becomes the means by which believers appropriate the gifts of salvation and participate in the relationship with the Father afforded us by Jesus in the Spirit. Whereas circumcision had formerly been the sign of identification as the people of God, now baptism becomes the rite of entrance into the *new* people of God.

Another integral aspect of the process of making disciples is teaching. In actuality, the teaching or instruction the disciples are to impart is Jesus himself. He—not the law—has become the new norm of morality and fidelity to God; in his person, he has embodied the essence of what it means to be a disciple. As the faithful Son of the Father and self-sacrificing brother to all peoples, he has taught us the meaning of commitment and love.

Finally, the great commission concludes with the assurance that those who become Jesus' disciples, who are incorporated into his life through baptism and learn from the teaching he himself embodies, will never want for his presence: "I am with you" (v. 20). Matthew's readers, with their rich Jewish heritage, would have been reminded of God's words of encouragement to all those whom he commissioned for service in his saving plan. To Moses, David and all the prophets, the same words, "I am with you," translated into courage and strength for the task at hand. Uttered by the risen Lord, this promise of presence brings the reader of the gospel full circle to the initial proclamation of good news in Matthew 1:23: "And they shall call him Emmanuel, a name which means 'God is with us.'"

These words represent both the joy and the mission of every baptized believer—to know and to live in the continued presence of the Lord and to be an aspect of that presence for all others.

Jesus' baptism

---

*O*riginator of the literary form known as gospel, Mark wrote the most abbreviated version of Jesus' saving mission. Because of this and the almost stark simplicity of Mark's style, the true genius of the first evangelist has been frequently undervalued.

Mark's particular portrait of Jesus (his christology) focused on Jesus' saving death and the redemptive value of his suffering. As Mark created his picture of Jesus as the suffering servant of God, he engaged his readers in a gradual realization that true Christian discipleship will also involve both suffering and service. Writing in the mid-to-late 60s, Mark provided strength and encouragement through his gospel for his contemporaries whose baptism into Christ had made them susceptible to the ever increasing threat of persecution.

In his short narrative about Jesus' baptism, Mark's primary concern was the revelation of Jesus' identity. At the outset of his gospel, Mark proclaimed Jesus as the Son of God (Mark 1:1); in Jesus' baptism, divine revelation underscores that identity. Only at the end of Mark's gospel, as Jesus completes his saving mission on the cross, will he again be so identified (Mark 15:39). Significantly, a Roman will make this final identification—a detail that no doubt strengthened the faith of Mark's predominantly Roman audience.

A scene filled with Old Testament themes, Jesus' baptism signaled the formation of a new Israel or a new people of God. The description of Jesus' coming up out of the water echoed the exodus from Egypt in which an enslaved Israel made a watery passage to freedom. As leader of the new Israel, Jesus will free from sin and death all who become identified with him through the waters of baptism.

Rent heavens were a familiar prophetic signal (e.g., Isaiah 64:1) that spelled the end of alienation and the beginning of a renewed communion between God and his people. In

Jesus the incarnate word, God would open the lines of communication in a wondrous and previously unimagined way.

Although artists for centuries have depicted Jesus' baptism scene with a dove as a representation of the Spirit, Daniel Harrington suggests that the dove be understood in a descriptive or adverbial sense, viz., "the Spirit descending dove-like." Just as a dove would hover before alighting on an object, so the Spirit hovered and rested upon Jesus. Calling to mind the Spirit that hovered over the waters at creation (Genesis 1:1), the scene at Jesus' baptism evoked the idea of a *new* creation: New life and rebirth were to come to humanity in the Spirit-empowered person and mission of Jesus.

Climactically, the voice from heaven clearly affirms the identity of Jesus as the Son of God. The first declaration, "You are my beloved Son," recalled texts in the Hebrew scriptures wherein the Son was identified as kingly and messianic (Psalm 2:7), as the only son of a loving father (Genesis 22:2), chosen specially for his task (Isaiah 44:2).

The second declaration, "On you my favor rests," identified Jesus as the servant of God (Isaiah 42:1) whose life would be spent in bringing light and justice to the nations. In the end, that servant whose qualities and mission Jesus epitomized was to suffer vicariously to free others from their sins.

Jesus' baptism served to identify his purpose and mission in life; the baptism of each Christian believer into Jesus' life and death serves a similar purpose.

Model citizens

Children should be seen and not heard." This old, familiar platitude no longer seems an apt description of the views of modern society toward its young. Ours has become a youth-oriented culture, and children are—for the most part—doted upon. In Jesus' day, however, the platitude rang true. Although they were regarded as blessings from God (Psalms 127, 128), children nevertheless had little status in society and virtually no rights as individuals. Therefore, the disciples' impatience with those who brought their children to Jesus is not surprising.

What *was* surprising, however, to the disciples and to Jesus' contemporaries was his response to the children and the lesson he taught through them. This short pericope is a pronouncement story, the point of which is made in Jesus' two sayings (vv. 15-16). It underscores the nature of the kingdom and the manner in which the kingdom is to be appreciated.

Contrary to the centuries-old expectation of his people that the kingdom would mean material blessings and political stability for Israel, Jesus challenged his contemporaries to recognize the kingdom as the reign (or will) of God, made manifest in his person and in his mission. Through his words and works, he made present and tangible the saving, forgiving and loving concerns of the Father for his sinful people.

Jesus' indignation toward his disciples was rooted in the fact that they had failed to perceive the true nature of the kingdom revealed in him. Had they been cognizant of that reality, they would not have prohibited the children access to Jesus. Not to be taken by storm or might, not to be claimed by virtue or right, the kingdom of God made present in Jesus is God's *free* gift to all who would receive it.

Jesus' indignation was also fired by the disciples' failure to recognize the children as "exemplary citizens" of the kingdom which he had made incarnate in their midst. Still innocent and trusting, children gratefully accept what is offered them in love. Humble and completely lacking in self-importance, children readily depend upon their parents and obey them without hesitation.

Not having learned to be suspicious of others' motives, children expect only the best from others. With resiliency and grace, children easily forgive and forget when wronged; they do not bear grudges or maintain a bitterness of heart. Because of their innate receptivity, children were blessed and praised by Jesus as models of discipleship in the kingdom he had come to bring. Their utter powerlessness enabled them to recognize and accept Jesus for who he was and to accept the kingdom as the gift that it is.

As Daniel Harrington has pointed out, the literature of the first century CE portrayed children as examples of unreasonable behavior or as objects in need of training. The gospel proclaims that children are to be taken seriously as persons. In later centuries, the church fathers who favored the practice of infant baptism cited this gospel text in support of their claims.

Today, all the baptized—regardless of their age—should strive to maintain that childlike trust and acceptance that enables the believer to recognize and accept the constant, caring gifts of God whenever, wherever and in whomever they are revealed.

Choosing wisely

Specialist par excellence in the Torah, the scribe who approached Jesus that day in Jerusalem could trace his spiritual ancestry to the priest-scholars who were exiled in Babylon in the sixth century BCE. In order to preserve the sacred traditions of Israel, these ancient scholars collected, copied and edited the scriptures, giving special care to the codification and interpretation of the law. In the period of reconstruction after the exile, those legal experts emerged as influential leaders in society, second only to the chief priests.

Highly respected and sometimes feared by their contemporaries, the scribes are usually cast in a dim light in the New Testament. Jesus berated them for their fascination with the external minutiae of the law and their seeming disregard for the interior dispositions that should motivate obedience to the law. In this pericope, however, the scribe appears in a uniquely favorable light because of his openness to Jesus and to the truth as it was revealed in him. Rabbis were frequently approached and asked their opinion as to the greatest law. The famous rabbi Hillel (whose school flourished 30 BCE - 9 CE) rendered this summation of the law: "What is hateful to you, do not do unto others. That is the whole Torah. All the rest is commentary. Go and learn." When Jesus was asked the same question, his response went far beyond Hillel's negative legislation concerning external behavior; Jesus delved into the realm of interior dispositions and motive, centered on the law of love.

By pairing Deuteronomy 6:4 (love of God) and Leviticus 19:18 (love of neighbor), Jesus distilled the law to its vital essence. Ezra Gould has suggested that Jesus' citing love of God as the first law is in itself a revelation of the very nature of God. Only one who loves can demand love, and only one in whom love is supreme can demand love as a supreme duty.

Moreover, the challenge to love God "with all your heart, with all your soul, with all your mind and with all your strength" underscored the unquantifiable quality of love. Such a love is incompatible with a legalism that defines limits; such a love is readily translated into the love of one's neighbor.

Mark is unique among the synoptics in narrating the scribe's reply to Jesus. Like the children who came, trusting and unassuming (Mark 10:13-16; see preceding commentary), and were received and blessed by Jesus, the scribe was well disposed and enthusiastic in his response. In contrast to the opinion of his fellow scribes who questioned Jesus' orthodoxy (Mark 3:22, 7:1-5), this scribe realized that Jesus' teaching was consonant with the sacred traditions of his people. Echoing Hosea 6:6 and 1 Samuel 15:22, the scribe understood that Jesus' call to love God and neighbor superseded any temple ritual. Sacrifice of animals—no matter how costly—and lavish rituals—no matter how well performed—could be simply perfunctory, external actions; but love requires a deliberate decision and the involvement of the whole person. By virtue of his insight, the scribe had drawn near to the kingdom, i.e., close to the mind and heart of Jesus himself.

On that note, Mark concluded his narrative (11:27—12:34) of the controversies between Jesus and the recognized authorities of his day. Mark observes that no one had the courage to ask him any more questions. Those who had debated with Jesus had encountered the truth in him; in the face of truth, there is no place for long harangues or debates. Each person who met Jesus found himself/herself in a crisis situation. The Greek *krisis* means "judgment" or "decision," and the corresponding verb *krinein* means "to sift" or "to separate."

Today, we who believe in Jesus meet him in the sacraments, in the sacred word and in one another. These encounters require the sifting and separating of ideas, values, beliefs and expectations—as well as a decision for or against Jesus. The scribe who met Jesus and chose wisely inspires us to similar insight and courage.

Born from above

Known as the Book of Signs, the first half of the fourth gospel (John 1:19—12:50) is structured around a series of seven signs. Each sign reveals something of Jesus' identity and mission, and challenges those who witness the sign to come to faith in him. According to this pericope, Nicodemus was aware of the signs Jesus was performing (John 3:2) and had come to investigate further. Perhaps Nicodemus was being mindful of the Midrash on Deuteronomy 18:19 which advised, "If a prophet who begins to prophesy [i.e., who is still uncredited] gives a sign and a miracle, he is to be listened to; otherwise he is not to be heeded" (Strack Billerbeck, II, 480).

Not mentioned in the synoptic gospels, Nicodemus is described in John's gospel as a Pharisee and a ruler (*archon*) in Israel. Recognized by Jesus as a teacher of Israel (John 3:10), Nicodemus had come to him by night. Some have suggested that Nicodemus' position within Jewish society may have warranted his cautious and furtive visit. Perhaps the nighttime designation is meant to reflect on Nicodemus' piety (fervent Jews were known for studying the law by night). More probably, the approach by night underscored a favorite Johannine motif, viz., the juxtaposition of light (as the realm of Jesus, truth and life) and darkness (as the realm of evil, sin and death).

In addition to the light-darkness motif (further expanded later in this episode, John 3:19-21), the encounter with Nicodemus is catalyzed by two other Johannine literary devices: ambiguity and misunderstanding. Each of these techniques fuels the pathos of the scene and provides the opportunity for further revelation by Jesus.

A faithful Jew loyal to the traditions of his people, Nicodemus believed that he and his fellow Israelites were intended, by virtue of their status as God's chosen people, to enjoy the reign or kingdom of God that the messiah would inaugurate. Jesus, however, challenged Nicodemus to a different perception of the kingdom or reign of God, the requisite for which would be not a *physical* birth into the Jewish race ("flesh begets flesh," John 3:16) but a *spiritual* rebirth from above ("Spirit begets spirit").

Because of the ambiguous nature of the term *anothen* (the word means "again" and "from above"), Nicodemus misunderstood, and the way was clear for Jesus to teach about the true nature of the kingdom as a share in eternal life, the favorite Johannine term for salvation (John 3:15-17). As Raymond Brown has pointed out, Nicodemus' knowledge of the Jewish scriptures should have enabled him to understand that Jesus was proclaiming the arrival of eschatological times when humankind would enjoy the status of children of God.

In order to enter God's kingdom, one must be begotten of water and the Spirit. Although Nicodemus may have understood the rebirth through water to refer to John the Baptizer's ministry of repentance and symbolic baptismal cleansing, later Christians associated the rebirth through water with the sacrament of baptism.

No doubt Nicodemus also remembered the promise of God preserved by Ezekiel: "I will sprinkle clean *water* upon you to cleanse you from all your impurities. . . . I will put *my Spirit* within you and make you live. . . . You shall be my *people* and I will be *your God*" (Ezekiel 36:25-28). The spiritual regeneration described in Ezekiel and elsewhere (Isaiah 59:21, Jeremiah 4:4, Joel 3:1f) was associated with the era of the messiah. Jesus' teaching and his challenge to Nicodemus underscored the fact that the messianic hopes of his people were being realized in him.

Evidently, Nicodemus' evening encounter with Jesus made an impact in his life. Later in the gospel, he appealed to the Jewish authorities that Jesus be treated with fairness (John 7:50-52). After Jesus' death, Nicodemus braved the Roman authorities to help in giving Jesus' body a respectable burial (John 19:39-42).

A prominent figure in ancient Christian art, Nicodemus was venerated as one who emerged from the darkness to approach the light of truth in Jesus. He remains a model for all who would be born from above through water and the Holy Spirit.

Living water

Animosity had characterized the interaction between Samaritans and Jews from as early as the eighth century BCE. After Assyria's conquest (722 BCE), the northern kingdom was colonized by foreigners from Babylonia and Medea; these colonists intermarried with those Israelites who had not been deported by the Assyrians. Because of this interracial background, the establishment of their own center of worship at Gerizim and their alliances with other nations, these Samaritan Jews were hated by their southern counterparts in Judah.

This centuries-old conflict is reflected in the surprised reaction of the Samaritan woman when Jesus asked her for water. In addition to this element of human prejudice, John's literary genius and theology vividly color the interchange between Jesus and the woman. In keeping with the evangelist's intention to portray Jesus as the effecter of a new beginning for all of God's people and as the one who would replace the institutions of Israel (law, temple, purification rituals, etc.) with himself, this episode at Jacob's well highlights Jesus as the new well-source from which all who thirst will receive eternal life.

Obviously, the woman had come to the well for water to quench her physical thirst. The unusual time (noon) has caused some to speculate that the woman purposely chose that hour in order to avoid the questions and/or comments of others, since the fact that the woman had had five husbands (John 4:18) may have made her seem less than reputable in the eyes of her fellow villagers.

Inviting her to satisfy more than mere physical thirst, Jesus challenged the woman to recognize the gift he could give and to ask him for *living* water (v. 10). Misunderstanding his offer, the woman responds (vv. 11-12) in a way representative of Johannine irony: Even without a bucket, Jesus was *indeed* greater than Jacob.

An ancient Palestinian Targum on Genesis 28:10 memorialized Jacob in this way: "After our ancestor Jacob had lifted the stone from the mouth of the well, the water bubbled to the top of the well, and was overflowing for 20 years!" Where Jacob's well had sustained the *physical* life of his people for centuries, Jesus supplanted Jacob in offering *living* water that would give *eternal* life.

Although theologians of the Middle Ages identified the living water (v. 10) as sanctifying grace received in baptism, there are a variety of more ancient suggestions as to the significance of Jesus' gift. In the sixth century BCE, Jeremiah (2:13) compared the *Lord himself* to a "source of living waters." In the eighth century BCE, Isaiah (12:3) called his people to draw water at God's *fountain of salvation.* Two centuries later, Deutero-Isaiah (Isaiah 55:1) extended God's invitation to all who thirst to "come to the water," to find the satisfaction of their needs in him.

Among the Essenes at Qumran, living water was a symbol for the Torah or *law.* Israel's wisdom literature made a similar association: "The *law* which Moses commanded us . . . it *overflows* with wisdom; it runs over, like the Euphrates" (Sirach 24:22-24). Therefore, as Raymond Brown concludes, Jesus' gift of living water was his teaching or revelation which replaced the law and enabled the thirsty to be satisfied with the incarnate wisdom of God himself in Jesus.

Jesus' gift of living water was also associated with the *Spirit.* The Greek Septuagint uses the special verb *hallesthai* ("leaping up," John 4:14) to describe the movement of God's Spirit which empowered Samson (Judges 13:25), David and other Hebrew heroes. Later in his gospel (7:38-39), John would clarify the association of Jesus' gift of living water with the Spirit.

In the figure of the Samaritan woman who came to the well to satisfy her thirst, the early Christians recognized a symbol of sinful humanity in need of God. By virtue of her encounter with Jesus, the source of living water, the woman became a witness to the truth she had learned in him (John 4:29, 39-42); through her, others came to believe. A popular baptismal motif in ancient Christian art, the woman's evolution from sinner *to* witness *epitomizes the power of grace—a power offered to each of us in every sacramental encounter with the Lord.*

Message and medium

*I*n the 1960s, the theories of the late Canadian educator, Marshall McLuhan (d. 1980), began to have an impact upon the global communications industry. The efforts of film makers, artists, photographers, authors, journalists and broadcasters were profoundly affected by McLuhan's basic premise, "The medium is the message."

Because the modern system of communication had evolved from static print to more fluid and varied media, care had to be taken to maintain a symbiotic relationship between the message and the manner through which that message was disseminated. Communicators faced the ever present pitfall that their message could be drowned out by a disconsonant or overpowering medium, or by a medium that offended the sensibilities of their audience.

In a sense, Jesus experienced a similar dilemma among his first century contemporaries. As the incarnate word of God, he was both the *message* God wished to speak to his people as well as the *medium* through which God made himself known. But Jesus was frequently rejected as an authentic message from God because he presented himself in a manner that confronted the prejudices and disappointed the expectations of his contemporaries. In the narrative immediately preceding this pericope, the Jews are presented as dismissing Jesus' message, complaining that they knew his origins. He was the son of Joseph! How could he pretend to come from the Father in heaven?!

Part of the bread of life discourse (John 6), this short text underscores the authenticity of Jesus' origins and his claim to be both medium and message of the good news of salvation. Because he is the one who has been sent by the Father, those who would know the Father must come to him. Indeed, the Father who wishes to be known by his children will *draw* them to Jesus. "To draw" (Greek *helkuein*) is the term used to describe the loving kindness (*hesed*) of God which attracts his people to him (Jeremiah 31:3). The rabbis used the same term in describing conversion as a "drawing near to the Torah."

As William Barclay has noted, "to draw" almost always implies some element of resistance. For example, *helkuein* is the verb used for *drawing* to shore a net heavy-laden with fish (John 21:6, 11). The same term described Paul and Silas' being *dragged* before the magistrates in Philippi (Acts 16:19).

In this pericope from John's gospel, the murmuring of the Jews (John 6:41-42) and their disbelief in Jesus constitute the element of resistance. If the Jews would heed Jesus' command to "stop your murmuring" (John 6:43), the Father would be able to draw them to Jesus to be nourished by the bread of his word and the bread of his very self.

Verse 45 represents a conflation of two prophetic texts (Isaiah 54:13 and Jeremiah 31:34), both of which challenge the murmuring and disbelieving to recognize the coming of the messianic era in Jesus and to become disciples with teachable dispositions; only then will they be able to *hear, learn* and *see* the Father in Jesus (John 6:45-46). For those who do allow themselves to be *drawn* to Jesus, his promise is one of eternal life (John 6:47) and resurrection on the last day (John 6:44).

Later in the gospel, Jesus will further explain that it will be in his being lifted up from the earth that he will ultimately *draw* all to himself (John 12:32). His death on the cross will be the climactic message of God's love and forgiveness for his people.

Baptism initiates the lifelong process of drawing near to the Father. The lines of communication are established. Those who would hear and see and know the Father must remain attentive to the message and the medium: Jesus Christ.

Come and drink

Every human life is punctuated by special times that celebrate the unique milestones and memories of that life. Every community marks special moments that have rooted and shaped and colored that community as a distinctive aspect of human society. Among the Jews, three major annual feasts sanctified their lives and times. One of those feasts—Sukkoth (Tabernacles, Tents, Booths)—forms the basis for this pericope and Jesus' solemn proclamation.

Originally an agricultural feast celebrated every autumn to give thanks for the harvest and to revel in its abundance, Tabernacles was eventually historicized in Israel and associated with the provident goodness of God during the wilderness period. During the seven days of the feast (an eighth day was added later), devout Jews lived in makeshift huts or tents (Leviticus 23:40-43) to remember the years spent traveling to the promised land.

Called by Josephus "the holiest and greatest festival among the Jews" (*Antiquities* 3:10:4), Tabernacles was a time for thanking God for his past, present and future blessings of water. Celebrants at the feast remembered God's gift of water from the rock in the desert (Exodus 17:6), thanked God for present sustenance and anticipated God's gift of rain to ensure future harvests.

During the feast, water from the pool of Siloam was carried daily to the temple. As the priest passed through the water gate, the people sang "with joy, you will draw water at the fountain of salvation" (Isaiah 12:3). Arriving at the temple, the priest poured the water on the altar; and the people, waving palm, myrtle, willow and citron branches, joined in prayer for God's continued blessings of life-giving water.

Within this context, on the last and greatest day of the feast, Jesus revealed *himself* as the source of living water. While the people of Israel thanked God for providing for their *physical* need for water, Jesus invited all who believe to come to him to satisfy their *spiritual* thirst for God.

By offering the gift of spiritual satisfaction, the Johannine Jesus challenged his contemporaries to remember similar offers God had made to his people in the course of salvation history and to understand that these offers were being realized in him (Isaiah 43:20, 44:3, 48:21). Years before John's gospel, Paul made it clear in his letter to the church at Corinth that the early Christians had come to identify Jesus as the rock that nourished the people of God: "And all drank the same spiritual drink, for they drank from a spiritual rock that followed them, and the rock was Christ" (1 Corinthians 10:4).

While not an exact citation of any one passage of scripture, v. 38 is probably based on the Jewish tradition preserved in Ezekiel 47:1-12 and Zechariah 14:8. Both prophets envisioned Jerusalem and the temple as a source of abundant, life-giving water flowing in all directions over the earth. Jesus' solemn proclamation, made in the temple on that great feast of Tabernacles, invited all to see that he supplanted both Jerusalem and the temple as the source of life.

Later in the gospel, at the moment of Jesus' entry into glory, the Johannine author will tell his readers that water (and blood) flowed forth from the side of the crucified Christ. The living water promised by Jesus to those who thirst and believe in him was released through the power of his saving death. In an aside (John 7:39), the evangelist explains that the living water refers to the Spirit, the experience of which would be afforded to believers only through Jesus' death and glorification (John 19:30, 20:22).

In baptism, those who believe come to Jesus, the source of living water, to be washed from sin and to satisfy every spiritual thirst. The Spirit empowers those who are washed in baptism to share in the life, death and resurrected glory of Christ himself.

One who has been sent

One of the many unnamed but attractive figures of the gospels is the man born blind, whom the early church revered as a model of faith and a patron of catechumens. Featured no less than seven times in the art of the catacombs, the man who received his sight from Jesus was also remembered in the writings of Tertullian, Justin Martyr and Augustine. As bishop of Hippo, Augustine wrote: "This blind man stands for the human race; if his blindness is infidelity, then his illumination is faith. He washed his eyes in the pool (Siloam) which is interpreted 'one who has been sent'; he was baptized in Christ."

Although the gift of sight to one who had been born blind was an astounding and wondrous event, the evangelist's description of the *physical* cure is simple and brief, comprising only two of the 41 verses of John 9. Sympathetic to his contemporaries' struggles in faith, the Johannine author chose to concentrate his efforts on the exploration of the man's *spiritual* healing. In successive and dramatic stages, the evangelist portrays the man's emergence from the *darkness* of ignorance and unbelief to a true and ever deepening knowledge of Jesus, the *light* of the world. In vivid contrast to the man's climactic profession ("I do believe, Lord," John 9:38) are the man's parents who feared to speak their minds for fear of the Jews, and the Pharisees whose *willful* blindness to Jesus' person and mission made them liable to judgment (John 9:23, 39-41).

A careful reading of the text with its references to expulsion from the synagogue (John 9:22, 33-35) reveals the fact that the evangelist has infused his narrative with issues pertinent to his contemporaries. In the last quarter of the first Christian century, Jewish Christians bore the brunt of increased persecution by the Jews who wished to purge what they perceived to be an heretical element. Therefore, those who professed Jesus as messiah were expelled from the synagogues. The man born blind, whose faith and spiritual insight into Jesus enabled him to withstand the cowardice of his parents and the scorn of the Pharisees, was a hero for the persecuted believers in the Johannine community.

This excerpted section of the narrative focuses on the contrast between life in Christ (signified by light) and a life of sin (signified by night and darkness). Having proclaimed, "I am the light of the world" (John 8:12), Jesus repeated that self-identification in John 9:5 and thereby challenged those in darkness to open themselves in faith to the healing and salvation he had come to bring. Reminiscent of the role of the servant in Isaiah 49:6, Jesus' cure of the blind man sent a clear message to his contemporaries that his was a mission of illumination and revelation. Rejecting the popular but incorrect notion that physical ailments were a punishment for sin, Jesus counseled his disciples to recognize the man's blindness as an opportunity for God's power to work through him. He also invited his contemporary and future disciples to join their efforts to his and so to share in his saving work of dispelling the darkness (John 9:4).

Significantly, the healing of the blind man was described by the evangelist as a process, involving clay, spittle, anointing or smearing of the "salve" on the eyes and a washing in water. Although these activities were regarded as a breach of the Sabbath's rest, nevertheless, Jesus—who had already claimed to share in God's power and authority to work on the Sabbath (John 5:15-20)—proceeded to manifest his power over sin and darkness by curing the man. Early baptismal rituals incorporated similar gestures, and the sacrament of baptism was referred to as "enlightenment" (Hebrews 6:4, 10:32; Justin Martyr, *Apologia* 1.61.12, 65.1).

Finally, by an exquisite paranomasia (play on words), the evangelist underscored the fact that the man's gift of sight was tantamount to an incorporation by faith into the very life and mission of Jesus. Throughout the fourth gospel, Jesus was described as the "one who has been sent" by the Father (John 3:17, 34; 5:36, 38; 6:29; 11:42; 12:49; 16:5; 17:3, 18, 21, and so on).

*B*y *directing the man to wash in the pool of Siloam and by the interpretation of the pool's name, "one who has been sent," the* *gospel invites believers to recognize their baptismal washing as a healing and an initiation into the very life of Jesus, the light of the world.*

The true vine

When the Johannine evangelist described the relationship by which Jesus and his disciples are bound to one another and to the Father, he chose an image well founded in the shared religious and political history of his contemporaries. The terraced, rocky slopes of ancient Israel were abundantly dotted with vines; and the entire process of planting, pruning and harvesting the grapes was a familiar and integral aspect of the people's daily experience. The image of the vine became a logical symbol for the nation and was ornately featured in the temple decor as well as on the coins minted during the Jewish revolt (66-70 CE).

Reflected also in the Jewish scriptures, the vine and/or the vineyard provided a rich and ready metaphor for illustrating the quality of life and conduct of God's chosen people. Occasionally, the symbol of the fruitful vine was employed to depict Israel's goodness and fidelity, as in Isaiah 27:2-6; but more often, the metaphor of a degenerate, spoiled and barren vine was used to represent Israel's unresponsiveness to God's lavish and constant care, as in Isaiah 5:1-7, Hosea 10:1-8, Ezekiel 15:1-8, Jeremiah 5:10-11 and 12:10-11. Only in light of these considerations can we fully appreciate the significance of Jesus' declaration, "I am the true vine."

Throughout his gospel, the fourth evangelist portrayed Jesus as replacing with himself the key elements of Judaism, its institutions, traditions and law. Here, within the context of the last supper discourse, Jesus is featured as replacing with himself the very nation of Israel, the chosen people of God. By calling himself the *true* vine, Jesus contrasted his own filial obedience and attentiveness to the Father with Israel's long record of infidelity and sin.

Because of the new relationship with the Father afforded to his people through Jesus, race or nationality or ancestral heritage would never again play a role in the process of salvation. Jesus' declaration made clear that union with him in loving, faithful discipleship constituted the new and true vine of the Father.

By the time the fourth gospel received its final form in the late 90s CE, believers had begun to understand that baptism was a means by which they were incorporated as branches into the true vine of Christ. Moreover, the other agricultural images of the vine and branches metaphor served as lessons for living their commitment to Christ.

Just as barren branches were pruned from the vine to allow it to flourish more abundantly, so would "barren" believers find themselves cut off from Christ and the community. And just as fruitful branches would also be trimmed in order to foster growth, so would faithful believers know the struggle of "being trimmed clean." For John's contemporaries, this pruning and trimming took the form of persecution from both the synagogue and secular authorities. Conflicts also arose within the community as differing factions struggled to maintain and promote their understanding of the gospel.

The term "clean" is also reminiscent of the foot washing event by which Jesus showed the extent of his love for his disciples. In washing their feet, he foreshadowed his death by which they would be ultimately made clean from sin and death.

In this particular pericope, Jesus assures his disciples, "You are clean already, thanks to the *word* I have spoken to you." As Raymond Brown has pointed out, there is no distinction in the fourth gospel between the saving word and the saving action of Jesus. Jesus and his revelation are virtually interchangeable. Therefore, because Jesus' "hour" (John 12:23) had already begun to unfold, Jesus' word or saving revelation was already at work within his disciples.

In order to remain "clean" and fruitful, Jesus' disciples were challenged to live on in him as he would live in them. An important theological concept in the Johannine writings, the term *menein* (live, remain, abide, stay, dwell) occurs over 65 times and expresses "the permanency of the relationship between the Father and Son and between the Son and the Christian" (R. Brown). Later theologians referred to this reality as "mutual indwelling" or the intimate and dynamic union which the Father and Son share with believers through the Holy Spirit.

Twenty centuries after his death and resurrection, Jesus' saving word continues to "clean" and to challenge those who live in him through baptism. This reality is the source of our confidence ("Ask what you will, it will be done for you"), of our love and obedience ("You will live in my love if you keep my commandments"), of our fruitfulness ("Who lives in me and I in him will produce abundantly") and of our joy ("That my joy may be yours and your joy may be complete"; quotes, respectively, from John 15:7, 10, 5, 11).

Blood and water

Rock of ages cleft for me,
Let me hide myself in thee;
Let the water and the blood
From thy side a healing flood,
Be of sin the double cure,
Cleanse me from its guilt and power.

With these words, the 18th-century defender of Calvinism, Augustus M. Toplady, set to music the profound theology of this pericope. Calling upon the richness of the Jewish faith by referring to the rock that sustained the life of Israel in the desert (Exodus 17:1-7), Toplady understood—as John did—that every hope for life and salvation was fulfilled in the moment of Jesus' death on the cross.

Unique to the fourth gospel, the particular details concerning Jesus' death addressed pertinent apologetic and theological issues within the Johannine community. Those details were: (1) the fact that it was Preparation Day, (2) Jesus' unbroken legs, (3) the piercing of Jesus' side, (4) the flow of blood and water, (5) the mention of an eyewitness.

As the evangelist would later explain (in John 19:36-37), the fact that Jesus' legs were not broken (the brutal Roman method of hastening death) was understood as a fulfillment of scripture. Passover legislation stipulated that the unblemished lamb to be offered was to be sacrificed without breaking its bones (Exodus 12:46, Numbers 9:12). Moreover, John's readers were aware that it was on Preparation Day that the priest began to sacrifice the lambs for the Passover feast. By alluding to these facts, the Johannine author portrayed Jesus as the Passover lamb par excellence, whose sacrifice would both effect and celebrate the ultimate exodus, freeing all peoples from their slavery to sin and death.

Also underlying the evangelist's narrative is the figure of the suffering servant "pierced for our offense, crushed for our sins . . . led like a lamb to the slaughter" (Isaiah 53:5, 7) as well as the shepherd-king featured in the prophecies of Zechariah. Though this messianic figure had come to pour out divine blessings on God's people, his leadership was rejected; he was thrust through, as the people looked on in mourning (Zechariah 11:12-14, 12:10).

John's portrayal of the crucified Jesus also served an apologetic interest. Docetism, with its claim that Jesus was not truly human, was posing a challenge to orthodox Christianity at the end of the first Christian century. By his emphasis on the flow of blood and water from Jesus' body, John underscored his true humanity. John's narrative also served to combat certain rumors that Jesus was not really dead but simply unconscious, and that he had been roused later by his disciples who claimed he had risen from the dead. Notice the fact that John brings together both the Jews and Roman soldiers as witnesses of Jesus' death.

For centuries, theologians have debated the meaning of the blood and water that flowed from Jesus' side; but medical, symbolic and miraculous explanations have fallen short of the one contained within the gospel itself. The clue lies in the claim of the eyewitness (probably the beloved disciple) who professed to tell the truth he knows "so that you may believe."

The blood that flowed from Jesus acknowledged the fact that his hour had come and, with it, the death through which he would be glorified. He is the good shepherd who would lay down his life for his sheep in order to take it up again; he is the Son of Man who was lifted up so that everyone who believes might have eternal life (John 10:15, 17; 12:24; 3:14-15).

The water that flowed from Jesus' side recalled his proclamation at the Feast of Tabernacles: "Let anyone who thirsts come to me and drink . . . as scripture says, 'Rivers of living water will flow from him.'" As the evangelist explained, "he said this in reference to the Spirit. . . . There was, of course, no Spirit yet because Jesus had not yet been glorified" (John 7:37-39). In Jesus' death and glorification, the Spirit has been poured forth to teach, to guide, to support and to strengthen his disciples forever.

Gradually the church fathers developed a secondary sacramental interpretation for the blood and water from Jesus' side: Eucharist (symbolized by Jesus' blood) and baptism (signified by the water) were understood as rooted in Jesus' sacrificial hour. Therefore, those who are baptized into Jesus are baptized into his death and resurrection. Those who share his eucharistic body and blood remember his death and celebrate his glory.

Special Readings

1 KINGS 17:17-24

Restored to life

The Rite of Baptism for Children supplies a "rite of bringing a child to the church" for those cases when an infant in danger of death has been hurriedly baptized and then recovers; this text from 1 Kings and the following one from 2 Kings are suggested for use in such situations.

Elijah's colorful story has been preserved in the first book of Kings. He spent most of his prophetic career as a foil to the infamous couple, Ahab and Jezebel. Son and successor of Omri, Ahab ruled Israel and dominated Judah in the ninth century CE. An excellent military strategist, Ahab was successful in fending off the Aramians and was the first Jewish king to engage Assyria in battle. So noteworthy was his prowess as a warrior that his name was inscribed on the monuments of that great opponent of Israel.

But Ahab was not favorably eulogized by the Deuteronomic historian because he permitted his Tyrian wife to practice and promote the cult of Baal in Israel. Though Ahab and Jezebel wielded the power of the throne among their people, it was Elijah whose fame spawned legends.

His power was from God and his authenticity was proven in the effectiveness of his ministry. Whatever Elijah prophesied came to fulfillment; every word he spoke in God's name was accomplished. This fact, as well as the belief in the Lord's superiority over Baal, form the framework for all of the stories concerning Elijah.

Prior to the raising to life of the widow's son, the power of Elijah's word had been proven in his prediction of the drought and in his promise of an unending food supply for the Sidonian woman and her son (1 Kings 17:1-16). In both instances, Elijah and the Lord appear as superior to Baal.

Baal was worshipped throughout the Syro-Palestinian world as a weather god with power to bring the rain and, with it, fertility for both fields and flocks. Jezebel had persuaded Ahab to build a temple and erect an altar to this Baal (1 Kings 16:32-33). Therefore, when Elijah's prediction of a drought became a reality and the ensuing famine threatened the lives of the people, it was evident that the prophet and the God whose word he spoke had no equals.

In this particular episode, the word of God spoken by Elijah is proven to be more powerful than death. The woman's questions reflect the popularly held belief that sickness and death were meted out as punishment for sin. Having experienced the goodness of God in Elijah, the woman was thereby overwhelmed with feelings of unworthiness. Blaming her own sin for her son's death, she regarded Elijah's presence as a reproach.

Interceding with the Lord on behalf of the woman and her son, Elijah was able to restore the boy to life. His action of stretching himself out over the boy three times may have been a recognized style of healing. Elisha (2 Kings 4:34, see next reading) and later Paul (Acts 20:9-10) would employ similar methods. But Jesus, whose power over life and death is prefigured in Elijah, will be shown as restoring another widow's son to life simply through the power of his *word* (Luke 7:11-16).

*B*y virtue of his encounter with Elijah, the dead boy was restored to life. The power of God was proven effective over death and sin. Restored to life, the boy was also restored to his mother. We Christians understand the sacrament of baptism as a similar encounter. Through it, we are touched by God. His powerful word effects life and forgiveness in us. Alive in God, we are also initiated into the life of that community which lives to bear witness to the power of his word.

Alert and hospitable

The Rite of Baptism for Children supplies a "rite of bringing a child to the church" for those times when an infant in danger of death has been hurriedly baptized and then recovers. This text from 2 Kings and the preceding one from 1 Kings are suggested for use in such situations.

Elisha, successor and heir to the prophetic ministry of his mentor Elijah, stands out as one of the great heroes of the Deuteronomic history. This so-called "history" comprises a series of biblical books (Joshua, Judges, 1 and 2 Samuel, 1 and 2 Kings) but it is actually a religious and theological *interpretation* of those people and events in Israel's story from the period of conquest to the fall of Jerusalem in 586 BCE.

A novice reader of this work might expect the kings of Israel and Judah to be the featured heroes. Given the fact that the temple was built during this period, one might also look to the institutional priesthood for a hero. But the Deuteronomic historian was more interested in the covenant God had made with Israel; every person and event was evaluated in terms of their fidelity or infidelity to that covenant. The successes Israel enjoyed as a nation were attributed to covenantal loyalty; likewise its failures in war, famines, etc., were seen as the result of breaches of the covenant.

The economic, political and military achievements of the kings were regarded as subordinate to their service to the covenant. In this regard, all of the kings of the northern kingdom were ranked negatively (e.g., "He did evil in the sight of the Lord," 2 Kings 13:2), while only three of Judah's kings received praise (e.g., "He pleased the Lord like his forefather David," 1 Kings 15:11).

Throughout this lengthy span of Israelite history, the only true heroes were those who were sent by God as emissaries of his word, the prophets. Speaking words of comfort and of challenge, bringing both promise and warning, the prophets were the constant guarantors of God's gifts of life and blessings for his faithful people.

In this wonderful narrative, the woman from Shunem is featured as a model of receptivity to God's word as revealed through the prophet. Having recognized the fact that Elisha was "a holy man of God" (2 Kings 4:9), the woman opened both her heart and her home to him. Her provision of a room complete with furnishings is an example of gracious oriental hospitality, reminiscent of that which Abraham provided for the three travelers at Mamre (Genesis 18). Just as Abraham received the unexpected reward of a promised son, so would the woman from Shunem be blessed for receiving the messenger of God's word. Recall the words directed toward Jesus' disciples in the gospel: "Whoever receives a prophet because he is a prophet will receive a prophet's reward" (Matthew 10:41).

When her child died, the woman displayed a trust and a resourcefulness born of true faith. Disregarding the customary protocol (pilgrimages to consult prophets were usually made only on holy days: 2 Kings 4:23), the woman went in search of the one man she knew could help her. Travelling the 25 miles to Mt. Carmel, she implored Elisha to come again to her home. Her confidence in initiating his prophetic activity did not go unrewarded. The power of God to give life to his people was at work in the prophet; the woman's son was restored to life.

As a baptismal lesson, this narrative reminds the believer of the necessity of being alert and "hospitable" to the word of God wherever, whenever and in whomever it is spoken. Those who are initiated into Christ's life through baptism are also challenged to search for the word of God, wherever that search may lead. In this regard, Jesus' words give us courage: "Ask and it shall be given to you; seek and you will find" (Matthew 7:7, Mark 11:24, Luke 11:9, John 11:22).

PART II

READINGS FOR WEDDINGS

First Reading

GENESIS 1:26-28, 31

The good creation

"*G*od looked at everything he had made and he found it very good." With this simple statement, the sixth century BCE priestly author provided readers with a profound and unparalleled commentary on his account of creation.

Telescoping four billion years of evolution into one "six-day" period, the author distilled centuries of thoughtful, faith-filled reflection into a poetic and theological presentation of humanity, its habitat, its relationship to God and to one another. This narrative intends neither science nor history; therefore, it does not follow nor meet the rules and expectations of scientists and historians. What this account gives us is theological insight; we are addressed not as skeptics or critics but as fellow believers. In one sense, the biblical account of creation could be called a celebration of all that the biblical authors had come to experience as true: The world is good; humanity is good. Human dominance and stewardship of the earth are God-given rights and responsibilities; human sexuality is an expression of divine goodness. Goodness—indeed, *very* goodness—is the basic and intrinsic quality of all of the created universe.

The biblical author illustrates humanity's noble and superior status in creation in several ways: (1) The account of human creation is the *climax* of God's creative work. (2) Humanity is created in the image and likeness of God. (3) The creation of humanity is portrayed as a *personal* act of God. Notice the fact that the creative command, "Let there be," has been replaced in this instance by "Let us make."

Debate continues concerning the identity of the "us" in v. 26. Some support the notion of a divine assembly, e.g., God, the heavenly hosts, angels, etc. Others point out that Elohim is a plural noun, reflecting the Semitic belief that God's divine state requires more than a *singular* expression. If this is the case, then "us" connotes the divine majesty of God. Still others see the term as a rhetorical device which may be simply understood in the sense of "Let's make" or "Let's do."

Of more importance is the notion of humanity created in God's image and likeness. Some have suggested that the Priestly author was referring to the spiritual aspect or human soul. But such an idea is an anachronism. The distinction between body and soul was a Greek idea; Hebrew anthropology viewed humanity as *nephesh*, a single living entity. The term "image" may refer to the ancient custom of sending a likeness or statue of the king to those areas of his realm he could not visit personally. If this is the intended meaning, then humankind may be understood as God's representative on earth. A further nuance of this interpretation may be found in the Priestly narrative itself. "Let us make man in our *image*" is clarified by the statement, "Let them have *dominion*." To be created in God's image is to have a share in God's power over all the created universe.

Finally, despite centuries of interpretative distortion, there is no basis in this narrative for the assumption of male dominance over the female. The Hebrew word for "man" which appears in vv. 26-27 is *'adam*—not a proper name or a reference to the male gender but a generic term for humanity.

Created in God's image, humanity is composed of both male and female aspects. Together, these share in God's dominion; together, they are neither subordinate nor competitive. Together, male and female are complementary and creative; together, these are "very good."

The two become one

---

*L*ike many of the stories in the primeval history (Genesis 1-11), the account of the creation of woman is an etiological narrative. In this particular story, the author's intention was to find foundation for and to explain the sexual attraction and complementarity that exists between men and women and that comes to fulfillment in the relationship of marriage. This etiology is similar to all the other etiologies in Genesis in that each communicates the author's fundamental belief, viz., that every aspect of existence finds its true and authentic meaning only when it can trace its origins to God. In this narrative, the attraction that draws man to woman and woman to man is raised above the level of base animal instinct and consecrated as a sacred, God-given gift.

Unlike the majestic and more ordered account of the Priestly author which was written later (sixth century BCE) but appears first in the book of Genesis, the earlier Yahwistic narrative (tenth century BCE) is more spontaneous and graphic; it focuses less attention on creation and more on the relationships that exist between women and men.

Given as the motive for the creation of woman is the divine observation, "It is not good for the man to be alone." Translated in English as man, the term *'adam* (v. 18) did not refer to a single individual nor was it originally a proper name. Rather, *'adam* with the definite article ("the") simply referred to the human being or humanity. Although none of the animals were suitable partners, the dominance of humanity over the animal world is shown in the fact that the human was empowered by God to name the animals. A suitable partner would not come from the animal world but from the same nature with which man had been endowed by God. The deep sleep or *tardemah* is always a biblical cue signalling divine intervention and/or a special revelation. In this instance, the deep sleep enjoyed by the man preserves the mystery of God's creative activity and communicates the wonder of the Genesis author as he contemplated the awesomeness of human existence.

The shared nature and complementarity of the male and female of the human species is illustrated in the description of the woman's formation from a rib of man. *Sela*, a word of uncertain meaning but traditionally translated as "rib," may also be related to a similar Sumerian word that means "life." The mutuality of man and woman is further supported by the proclamation that she is "bone of my bones and flesh of my flesh." In Hebrew, the divinely ordained partnership is orchestrated in a paranomasia or wordplay: Man (*'ish*) and woman (*'ishshah*) are meant to be together as partners in a relationship that supersedes even the blood bonds shared by parents and their children. The last phrase of this reading underscores the covenantal quality of the marriage relationship: "The two of them become one body."

Today, even with a divorce rate at more than 50 percent, marriage remains a mysterious but precious union. In his book, The Warrior, the Woman and the Christ, *G. A. Studdert-Kennedy described it in this way: "Love is the joyous conflict of two free, self-conscious persons who rejoice in one another's individualities and . . . through the clash of mind on mind and will on will work out an ever increasing but never finally completed unity."*

Isaac and Rebekah

---

*I*n *Fiddler on the Roof*, the character Yenta renders a humorous and often unappreciated service. A matchmaker of dubious skills, Yenta made her living pairing men and women for marriage in the small village of Anatevka. More recently, the movie *Crossing Delancey* featured a similar character who successfully brought together the unlikely couple of a downtown New York pickle-maker and an uptown literary assistant. Arranged marriages have been an accepted if not always popular practice in many of the world's cultures—but the arrangements in the pairing of Rebekah and Isaac are singularly special. According to the Yahwistic author, *divine* choice and *divine* promise guide the entire matchmaking process.

Omitted from this excerpted pericope is the fact that Abraham, concerned for the preservation of the family line and mindful of God's promise of progeny, sent his servant to find a wife for Isaac. Unwilling to allow Isaac to marry a Canaanite woman whose influence could diminish the rich heritage of the faith among his people, Abraham looked to his own clan for a suitable bride for his son. As he journeyed, the servant prayed that God would assist his search by means of a sign, viz., that the woman from whom he would request water would respond favorably and offer to water his animals as well. The servant's prayer was realized in the person of Rebekah. Her generous and nurturing character shone through as she saw to the needs of Abraham's servant and his caravan of ten camels. Convinced that he had found a wife suitable for Isaac, the servant made a formal request for Rebekah. The fact that the arrangements were made with her brother Laban, rather than her father Bethuel, indicated that Bethuel was either dead or too feeble to transact the business at hand. Laban's statement, "This thing comes from the Lord" (v. 50), was a response to the servant's account of his request for a sign and of Rebekah's actions. Also included in the statement is the Yahwist's belief that what was transpiring was according to God's plan for his people. The blessing invoked for Rebekah (v. 60) further illustrates this conviction and reminds the reader that God's promises to Abraham would continue to be fulfilled (Genesis 22:17) in the union of Rebekah and Isaac.

Ordinarily, the consent of the bride-to-be was not required in an arranged marriage but, in this instance, Rebekah was consulted (v. 58). Some cultures (Nuzi) required bridal consent if the marriage was arranged by someone other than her father; others (Assyrian) protected the woman's option to remain in her homeland. Perhaps one or both of these customs were respected in Aram Naharaim.

When Rebekah, the servant and their entourage arrived in the Negeb, Isaac was "out . . . in the field" (v. 63). While some translations, including the NAB, choose not to translate the obscure Hebrew term used in this verse, the KJ and RSV tell us that Isaac was "out *meditating* in the field." The JB simply says he was "*walking* in the fields." Others have suggested that the term was a euphemism for answering the call of nature. However, the idea of Isaac meditating would coalesce with the Genesis author's habit of portraying the patriarchs of his people in the most favorable light.

Would-be brides and grooms of this century need not rely on the services of matchmakers nor need they submit to an arranged marriage. But there is a lesson in this charming story of Rebekah and Isaac. She was chosen not for her looks or dowry but for her noble and generous character. Isaac took time to go out and meditate. Though their subsequent life together was not without its trials (Rebekah was initially barren, and Jacob and Esau wrote the book on sibling rivalry!), nevertheless, Isaac is the only patriarch who remained monogamous. Obviously, there is something to be said for character and contemplation.

Made in heaven

*M*ove over, Garrison Keillor! The anonymous author of Tobit is unparalleled in his ability to weave romance, high adventure, folklore and moral imperative into a story that has edified and entertained both Jews and Christians for over two millennia.

Written somewhere in the diaspora (possibly Egypt) in the late third or early second century BCE, the book of Tobit represents a Jewish reaction to the increasingly pervading influence of Greek culture. As such, it portrays upright Jewish characters whose lives testify to the belief that true wisdom is to be found only in the rich heritage of Israel. A didactic fiction, the book was meant to encourage Jews in the diaspora to remain faithful to their orthodox traditions and family values. To that end, intermarriage with gentiles was discouraged; and the corporal and spiritual works of mercy, prayer, fasting and almsgiving were idealized in the story's main characters.

The narrative is set in the late eighth century BCE within a community of Jewish exiles deported to Nineveh (Assyria) after the fall of Israel. Featured are two families, both of whom have maintained an upright and holy family life despite the attraction of foreign ways. Each of the families has had its share of life's struggles. Tobit, after a series of severe reversals, was struck blind; his wife Anna had to seek work as a weaver in order to support the family. As Tobit prays for death, the author transports the reader to Medea to witness the trials of another Jewish family. There Raguel, Edna and their daughter Sarah were tormented by a wicked demon named Asmodeus. According to the story, Sarah's parents were seeking an *eighth* husband for their daughter because her first seven had been killed on their wedding night by Asmodeus! Sarah, meanwhile, was praying for death.

When God heard the desperate prayers of both Sarah and Tobit, he sent Raphael, an angel messenger, whose commission to heal both Tobit and Sarah would bring their two families together. As a result of God's intervention through Raphael (called Azariah in the story), Sarah and Tobiah (Tobit's son) are united in marriage and live "happily ever after." This joyous resolution to what appeared to be two impossible situations illustrates the author's basic intention, viz., to affirm God's protective, provident presence in the everyday lives of his faithful people, wherever and whenever they are in need.

This excerpt details the actual wedding ceremony of Tobiah and Sarah whom Raphael had earlier described as the one "set apart for you [Tobiah] before the world existed" (Tobit 6:18). The notion of God's guiding the unions of his people is affirmed here in Raguel's statement, "Your marriage . . . has been decided in heaven!" (Tobit 7:11). These references, as well as several other details (Tobiah's journeys, the refusal of hospitality until the wedding was arranged, the fact that a mate was sought from the same clan) serve to associate the relationship of Tobiah and Sarah with those of the great Israelite patriarchs and their wives (Genesis 24 and 29).

The wedding ceremony seems to follow the pattern of marital contracts found among fifth century BCE Elephantine papyri found in Egypt. Signed and sealed marriage contracts were not customary in Israel, nor is such a practice stipulated in Mosaic law; however, Jews in the diaspora did observe such practices.

Notice that the ceremony was concluded by a meal. The author's simple statement, "Afterward they began to eat and drink" (Tobit 7:15), invites us to consider marriage as a covenantal union in which both parties call upon God to witness their love and to sustain their commitment. Like all covenants, the shared meal bound those who partook of it to one another for life.

Trustful prayer

Some scholars have compared the book of Tobit to a literary genre that we have come to enjoy: the fairy tale. Tobit *does* exhibit that fairy tale quality which J. R. R. Tolkien called "eucatastrophe" or "the happy resolution of a desperate situation." Nevertheless, despite its occasional dalliance in the world of imagination, Tobit delivers an extremely serious message. Like the Deuteronomic historian, the author of Tobit wishes to edify and encourage his people to remain faithful to the covenant. Therefore, desperate situations (like the exile) were to be accepted as punishment for covenantal infidelity, and happy resolutions (like the return from exile and the restoration) were to be enjoyed as a result of the people's reconciliation with a merciful, caring God. This theological perspective is summed up in Tobit's prayer of praise (Tobit 13).

This particular pericope presents us with another prayer, that of Tobiah and Sarah on their wedding night. (For a brief summary of the events that transpired up to this point, see the commentary, above, on Tobit 7:9-10, 11-15.) Through God's intervention by the angel Raphael, Tobiah was able to break the tradition of death that had plagued Sarah's seven former marriages. Following Raphael's instructions, Tobiah placed the liver and heart of a fish on the embers for the incense (Tobit 6:17-18). Repulsed by the odor, the demon fled the bridal chamber whereupon Raphael chased him into the desert of Upper Egypt and bound him there (Tobit 8:1-3). The desert was believed to be the habitat of evil spirits, demons, etc. Such methods for dealing with evil spirits were commonplace in the ancient world, but it is clear that the author of Tobit gave greater import to the intervention of God and the power of prayer.

After the demon Asmodeus had gone, Tobiah (again following Raphael's instructions) invited Sarah to pray with him. Prayer to God is a crucial aspect of the entire book of Tobit.

The featured characters are portrayed in prayer at every important juncture of the story. For example, when his life situation seemed unbearable, Tobit prayed to God for the deliverance of death (Tobit 3:2). Sarah prayed similarly after being widowed for the seventh time (Tobit 3:11-15). Later in the story, Tobit would thank God in prayer for his restored sight (Tobit 11:14-15). The entire book climaxes with a prayerful celebration of God's care (Tobit 13:1-18).

The prayer of Tobiah and Sarah recalls the wondrous gift of the creation of the universe and of humanity (Adam and Eve), and understands the union of Tobiah and Sarah as an integral part of God's creative purpose for his people. Tobiah identifies his motives as noble and not lustful, and asks God's blessing and mercy on their life together. Sarah's response, "Amen" (Tobit 8:8) is the only word she speaks in the presence of another human being in the entire book. All her other words were in the form of private prayer to God.

At this point in the story, sorrow evaporates, and the newlyweds and their respective families experience God's blessings and lasting joy. The message for the author's contemporaries was clear: Reliance on God in trusting prayer would see his faithful people through any trial. The message for our contemporary society is equally clear: Relationships with God and with one another, especially the relationship of marriage, become stronger and more lasting if supported by sincere and frequent prayer.

Human love

*I*n one of his so-called "supper sermons," Martin Luther expounded on his opinion that sex of itself leads to lust rather than to love. According to the great reformer, "The reproduction of mankind is a great marvel and mystery. Had God consulted me in the matter, I should have advised him to continue the generation of the species by fashioning them of clay." Despite his clever repartee, Luther's ideas about sexual love are alien to those represented in the biblical book called Song of Songs.

An anthology of love songs and/or poems of disputed date and unknown authorship, Song of Songs is filled with provocative images and graphic metaphors that celebrate human love and the romantic expression of that love by both its male and female counterparts. Anyone who reads this unusual book (there are 49 *hapax legomena* in 117 verses!) will agree that the authors have succeeded in their poetic purpose, i.e., "to transfuse emotion, not to transmit thought but to set up in the reader's senses a vibration corresponding to what was felt by the writer" (A. E. Houseman). Hugh T. Kerr describes Song of Songs as "a ministry of love" and urges the reluctant to allow themselves to learn the book's central lesson of love: Love is stronger than death! Although God is never mentioned in the book, the authors reflect the view put forth elsewhere in Hebrew wisdom literature, viz., that human love is a divine gift to be enjoyed within the context of a faithful and exclusive relationship (Proverbs 5:15-21, Ecclesiastes 9:9).

After considerable debate, Song of Songs was accepted into the Hebrew canon of scripture (ca. 90 CE), but only after Rabbi Akiba interpreted the love relationship explored in the book as that between God and Israel. Other interpreters have made similar attempts to sublimate the book's basic message. Origen, for example, encouraged Christians to understand Song of Songs as an allegory on the relationship between Christ and the church. Bernard of Clairvaux preached 86 sermons in this regard. The great mystic John of the Cross understood this wisdom work as an analogy of the relationship between Christ and the soul of the believer. Others have suggested that the book features Wisdom as a passionate lover, enticing those who seek her to pursue her relentlessly. Still others, especially in the Roman Catholic tradition, have proposed that the feminine protagonist in the book is the Virgin Mary because her life was one of exemplary union with God (therefore, excerpts from the book are featured on Marian feasts).

Although these several attempts at interpretation have pedagogical and inspirational value, most serious scholars agree that the original significance of Song of Songs is found on the level of romantic human love. Remarkably, the woman depicted in these poems is an exceptional character. Contrary to the patriarchal culture within which the work was written, she is not subordinate to man but is his full partner. Their relationship is one of balance and not dominance, of passionate mutuality and not enmity. Renita Weems suggests that readers accept Song of Songs as the authors' critique of their culture as well as a critique of those scriptural texts that seem to accent the disharmony between man and woman and to penalize the free expression of feminine sexuality as a source of sin.

In the enduring, faithful and passionate relationship shared by the woman and man in Song of Songs, Thierry Maertens and Jean Frisque have identified a microcosm of the kingdom of God. According to these scholars, "The kingdom of God is not the one-dimensional universe towards which our reasonable shallow society tends. We find it whenever two human beings begin to understand one another, to respect and to love one another." In the mutual love and self-giving that is marriage, the kingdom of God is reflected and the people of God experience the goodness of their creator.

Gift and blessing

Longest of all the sapiential books, the Wisdom of Jesus ben Sira (also called Sirach and Ecclesiasticus or Book of the Church) is a compilation of proverbs, maxims and instructions written in Hebrew in the early second century BCE (ca. 180). It was the author's intention, and later that of his grandson who translated the work into Greek, to address and alleviate the struggles of faithful Jews living in the diaspora. Attracted by the growing influence of Greek culture and philosophy, Jews were hard-pressed to retain their traditions and maintain the integrity of their religious beliefs.

Sirach encouraged his contemporaries to remain faithful to the Lord, source of all wisdom (Sirach 24:1-21), and to the expression of God's wisdom in the Torah or law (Sirach 24:22). This same preservationist and traditionalist spirit which pervaded ben Sira's work would ignite the Maccabean revolt less than two decades later.

According to this wisdom author, the key to attaining true wisdom, and thereby true happiness, is "fear of the Lord" (Sirach 1:4). "Fear" in the biblical sense means that fundamental attitude of reverence and awe for God which is translated into true worship and right moral living. Those who fear the Lord and thus attain true wisdom will be blessed. In this particular reading, the blessing (Sirach 26:3) takes the form of a good wife!

Part of a longer pericope that compares wicked and virtuous women (Sirach 25:13 - 26:18), this particular text understands the value of a woman as relative only to what she can do and/or be for her husband. Nevertheless, she is called a blessing and a gift who brings joy and fulfillment to her mate. Feminists may bristle at this domestic and servile description of women's role but Sirach was not unique in his attitude. On the contrary, most of the ancient Near Eastern cultures shared similar ideas about women's place in society. Rather than blame the ancient authors for a mentality they reflected but did not create, it is better perhaps to take a broader view of the ever evolving biblical society. Indeed, rabbis of the same generation taught their people: "He who has no wife lives without good or help or joy or blessing or atonement; he is not really a complete man, he diminishes the divine likeness."

As he draws attention to the positive value of a good wife, notice that the author praises her for thoughtfulness and virtue. These are precisely the qualities that promote and sustain the lasting union of marriage. Wealth or the lack of it is not a gauge of happiness. Contentment is found in the person of a good woman.

It is significant that the author describes the wife in terms of a "generous gift" from God and as a "blessing" of "surpassing worth." If the one with whom we form a marriage bond is valued and cherished as a gift and a blessing, the relationship will be a healthy, holy and happy one. Then marriage can be appreciated and lived as a covenant rather than a contract.

From the heart

When Jeremiah was called to minister as the Lord's prophet, he was commissioned "to root up and to tear down, to destroy and to demolish, to build and to plant" (Jeremiah 1:10). Throughout his prophetic career, Jeremiah worked relentlessly at rooting up and tearing down the barrier that human sin had erected between God and his people. His words were harsh and his style blunt as he warned his contemporaries of the inevitable outcome of their idolatry and infidelity.

But in this particular pericope, the tone of the prophet's message reached its most sublime level; with these words, Jeremiah fulfilled his mandate "to build and to plant." Called "the gospel before the gospel" (Stanley R. Hopper), "one of the mountain peaks of the Old Testament" (James P. Hyatt), as well as "the apogee of all prophecy" (Guy Couturier), these few verses soothed the wounds of a shattered people during the exile and stirred their hopes and expectations for centuries after Jeremiah's death.

At the heart of Israel's dealing with their God was the covenant or relationship initiated by the Lord. Through Moses' mediation, God had promised Israel, "If you listen to my voice and keep my covenant, you shall be my special possession, dearer to me than all other people" (Exodus 19:5) and "You shall have me as your God" (Exodus 6:7).

The terms of the covenant, the decalogue, were carved in stone as a permanent reminder and challenge (Exodus 31:18, 34:28). By observing the law, the people were assured of their continued bond with the Lord. But as the Jewish scriptures attest, a faithless Israel had repeatedly breached the covenant. Without the covenant, Israel was virtually bereft of a future. Therefore, Jeremiah's promise of a *new* covenant was tantamount to an offer of new life.

Like his prophetic colleagues, Jeremiah called for an interiorization of the terms of the covenant: "I will place my law within them and write it upon their hearts." Jeremiah recommended an "ethic not based on the sanction of an external law or on human effort, but on communion with God at the deepest level of the self" (Thierry Maertens and Jean Frisque). For the biblical authors, the *heart* is the seat of human intelligence and will. Jeremiah had been prolific in condemning the hardheartedness or recalcitrance and self-sufficiency of his people (Jeremiah 3:17, 7:24, 9:13, 11:8, 13:10, 16:12, 18:12, 23:17) which had led to their alienation from the Lord. He who had declared, "The sin of Judah is written with an iron stylus, engraved with a diamond point upon the tablets of their hearts" (Jeremiah 17:1), now promised the gift of a heart divinely engraved with God's own will and purpose for his people. This covenant would be *new* in the sense that the same God who initiated it and dictated its terms would also put into the hearts of his people the *power* to respond to him in faithfulness and love. Later theologians would give to this *new heart* or *new power* the name of "grace."

Comparable to Ezekiel's vision of a new heart and a new spirit for Israel (Ezekiel 11:19, 18:31, 36:26), Jeremiah's promise found its fulfillment in the new covenant with God sealed by Jesus' blood (Luke 22:20, 1 Corinthians 11:25). Using this text from Jeremiah as a foundation, the author of the letter to the Hebrews made an extensive comparison of the old and new covenants (Hebrews 8:7—10:17); this comparison enables Christians to trace their relationship with God to its Jewish roots and to find its full flower in Jesus' person and mission.

Jeremiah's vision of the new covenant encourages all who enter into relationships to maintain an integrity such that exterior behavior is a sincere expression of interior reality. Those relationships that spring from purely external attractions and that are bound solely by exterior contractual obligations and/or sanctions will die. Only those relationships that are formed and fostered within the "heart" (viz., those based on grace and knowledge and motivated by good will) will flourish and endure.

Wisdom's rewards

*S*WF *in mid-40s seeks SWM 40ish or 50ish with interests in sports, nouvelle cuisine, rap and reggae. Call 555-1234; will answer all responders.*

Newspaper or magazine ads such as this one have become commonplace in contemporary society as people become more creative in their search for significant relationships. Some dating services have gone "high tech," helping hopeful clients produce video presentations of themselves and their description of an ideal mate.

At first glance, this text from Proverbs may sound like such a description. Indeed, the woman whose virtues are herein detailed would certainly seem to be a warm and worthy companion. But, in actual fact, the author of Proverbs intended this poem to portray more than a wonderful woman. This paragon of virtue—skilled and industrious, concerned for her own as well as for the poor and the needy—is none other than Wisdom personified.

In both Hebrew (*hokmah*) and Greek (*sophia*), "wisdom" is a feminine noun, therefore Wisdom's personification has been characterized in a feminine manner. Earlier in Proverbs, Wisdom was portrayed as building a house and preparing a sumptuous banquet to which she invited the simple, those lacking in understanding and those who would become more wise. To all who would seek her, Wisdom promised long life and knowledge of God (Proverbs 9:1-16). In this, the last chapter of Proverbs, the author describes the blessed and secure existence Wisdom provides for those who have spent their lives in search of her. Like the contented husband of a good wife, those who commit themselves to wisdom will know happiness, prosperity and a good reputation among their peers.

A compilation of proverbs and instruction, representing both early (monarchic) and late (exilic and post-exilic) material, the book called Proverbs probably received its final editing during the late sixth or early fifth century BCE. Similar in character to the rest of Israel's sapiential literature, Proverbs endorses a strict monotheism, the highest ethical standards and the principle that true wisdom comes from faithful observance of the law.

Whereas the Pentateuch taught the lessons of moral living through legislation, and the prophets through exhortation, Proverbs educates by inviting the readers to reflect on their life experiences and to apply the lessons learned toward shaping a more upright existence.

While Israel struggled with the attractions of foreign philosophies and cultures, its native sages encouraged their people to come home to Yahweh and to the "hearth" of the law and the covenant where they had been born and reared as a people. There they would learn true and authentic wisdom.

The woman of worth described by the Proverbs' author is a model whose virtues challenge all believers—male and female. She exemplifies that insight which sees beyond charm and beauty (v. 30) and penetrates with awe and faith ("fear of the Lord," v. 30) into the mysteries of God. As such, she is to be sought after and revered by all who seek sincere and lasting relationships with the Lord and with one another.

Second Reading

ROMANS 8:31-35, 37-39

The power of God's love

Years ago, when my husband and I were preparing the ceremony that would express and celebrate our marriage, we agreed that this excerpt from Paul's letter to the Romans should be included. We believed that finding one another (we come from two different continents and met on a third) had been a divine and providential gift, and that our shared faith in God would be our best asset. At that time, one out of every two marriages ended in divorce; nevertheless, we were certain that our love for one another was a sign of God's love for us, and we hoped that nothing would ever prove to be more powerful. In a sense, this is the same certainty Paul wished to communicate to the Christians in Rome.

Paul did not found the church in Rome but he was familiar with the situation there, as his letter attests. Politically, Christians were held suspect by the Roman civil authorities who regarded them as poor candidates for citizenship. Besides ascribing to a faith considered illicit by Rome, Christians refused to take part in Roman feasts and to worship the emperor. Conflicts flared as conservative Christians of Jewish origin denigrated the faith of gentile Christians and attacked those who had evangelized them as having diluted the gospel for their benefit. As a result of these difficulties, Christians often found themselves to be the scapegoats in a hostile environment. Aware of their struggles, Paul elaborated for the Romans the advantages and blessings which were theirs by virtue of their life in Christ. This pericope represents the culmination of Paul's argument and is a veritable celebration of the love of God which far outweighs any burden the believer may experience.

Using language befitting a courtroom, Paul posed a series of rhetorical questions to the Roman Christians: "Who can bring a charge against God's chosen? . . . Who shall condemn?" Citing God as the believer's supreme advocate ("God is for us"), Paul swept away all other opposition with the reminder that God had given his Son for us. If Christians have already been the recipients of such magnanimous love, how could there be any doubt as to God's continuous care and concern? The reference to "all things besides" recalled for Paul's readers the gifts he had previously listed in Romans 8, viz., glory (v. 18), revelation of the children of God (v. 19), freedom (v. 21), adoption as children of God (v. 23), redemption of our bodies (v. 23), the Spirit's help and intercessions (v. 26) and the promise that all these things will work together for the good of those who love God (v. 28). In addition to the gift of divine advocacy, the believer has been justified by the death of Christ who continues to intercede for us at the Father's right hand.

To further strengthen his case, Paul then listed a variety of calamities, both natural and supernatural, and dismissed each in turn, as having been conquered by the love God has for his people. Angels, principalities and powers refer to the ranks of heavenly beings who, according to the rabbis, resented God's creation of humanity and were, therefore, "grudgingly hostile" to humans (W. Barclay). Height and depth were astrological terms referring to stars at their rising ("height") when their influence over humanity was thought to be greatest, and at their nadir ("depth") when their power was believed to begin to build once again. Not limited by any dimension ("neither the present nor the future"), the love of God upholds the believer in this life, and assures the same passage through death to glory ("neither death nor life") which has been travelled by Jesus.

Over, above and beyond all these real and/or supposed powers, Paul promised victory ("we are more than conquerors") to those who believe in Christ and are loved by God. No doubt God affords the same victory to those whose pledge of love to one another is centered on and rooted in him.

Advice and challenge

Paul was an excellent educator; he was capable of leading his readers to the heights of theological truth as he shared his profound insight into the mystery of the Christ-event. But he never left his charges dangling in speculation. In each of his letters, Paul issued *practical* advice and very real *challenges* to aid his readers in translating their professed faith into their everyday lives. This excerpt from Romans is a fine example of Paul's talent for exhortation and parenesis.

Paul appealed to his Roman readers to find their motivation for living in the "mercy of God" (v. 1) which had been repeatedly manifested to them. The ultimate manifestation of divine mercy became incarnate in the person of Jesus Christ by whose saving death all who believe are justified, i.e., brought into a right relationship with God.

This unmerited gift of salvation and reconciliation called forth from the very heart of the believer only the noblest and most authentic response. Paul understood that this response was not to be dictated from without by laws or sanctions; on the contrary, he regarded the Christian ethic as a lifestyle inspired and structured from within the loving relationship the believer shared with Christ by the power of the Spirit.

For this reason, Paul implored the Romans to move beyond a mere external conformity to the world ("this age," v. 2) and to be transformed unto Christ from within ("by the renewal of your minds," v. 2) so as to understand the will of God. Elsewhere in his letters, Paul portrayed this aspect of the Christian ethic as being dead to sin and alive to God in Christ (Romans 6:11), as "being in Christ" (2 Corinthians 5:17), being "clothed with Christ" (Galatians 3:27) and as "having the mind of Christ" (Philippians 2:5).

Here, in his letter to the Romans, Paul describes the life of the committed believer as genuine prayer ("a living sacrifice of spiritual worship," v. 1). Then in a series of several maxims (vv. 9-18), Paul outlined the manner in which the believer's spiritual worship would be manifested in the routine interactions of human existence.

Similar to the teachings and sayings of Jesus gathered into the great sermon by Matthew (5:1-7:27) and by Luke (6:20-49), Romans 12:9-18 delineate the Christian's vocation to live in counter-culture to the world. Love for enemies, patience in trial, a ban on ambitiousness and a call to lowliness—all of these challenges were, of course, met by Jesus and were to be shouldered by his would-be disciples. For the self-centered and the self-indulgent, Paul's exhortation probably seemed like pious drivel at worst, and at best an impossible ideal. Nevertheless, this was the life-style required of all who realized themselves to be beneficiaries of God's gracious mercies.

Paul's maxims are both Christocentric and altruistic. Just as these practices and attitudes would foster a vital and loving community life among Christian disciples, so also will they forge viable and durable marriage bonds and familial relationships.

Harmony

*A*ccording to the *American Heritage Dictionary*, Second College Edition, *harmony* is a "pleasing combination of musical elements that blend to form a whole." Etymologically, however, "harmony" was originally a term used, not by musicians but by carpenters. From the Greek *harmozein*, the word referred to the ability of craftsmen to "fit together" various pieces of wood into an object of usefulness and beauty.

When Paul called for *harmony* (Romans 15:5) within the Roman church, he was, in effect, challenging each unique, individual believer to allow his/her distinctive ideas, talents and opinions to blend with those of others to form a beautiful whole. In this particular instance, the "beautiful whole" was the united community of Christian believers in Rome.

A variety of issues threatened the unity of Rome's mixed population of Jewish and gentile Christians. Disagreements with regard to dietary practices (Romans 14:21), debates concerning the eating of food which had been sacrificed to pagan gods (Romans 14:2, 14) and the observance of certain feasts (Romans 14:5-6) had divided the community into two major factions which Paul called the "weak" and the "strong." Although he personally identified with the latter group, Paul exhorted both factions to avoid: (1) mutual criticism, Romans 14:1-12, (2) giving scandal, Romans 14:13-23, and (3) selfishness, Romans 15:1-13.

Christ and his selfless example of altruistic love should be the ideal upon which each community member should model his/her behavior. Just as "Christ did not please himself" (Romans 15:3) but was the consummate man for others, so must those who believe in him live to please and support one another in faith. The phrase, "put up with" (v. 1), is not the best rendering of the Greek verb *bastazein*. To "put up with" the failings of another seems to advise mere passive tolerance, however. The verb actually calls for the more positive action of bearing another's burdens and shouldering their cares so as to better their lot and thereby build up the community as a whole.

When the strong bear the burdens of the weak, and the weak live to please their neighbor, then there is harmony within the community. It is significant that Paul advocated *harmony* and not *conformity* or *uniformity*. He realized from personal experience that faith in Christ could unite even the most disparate minds in a fundamental harmony. Harmony does not imply complete agreement, nor does it even preclude heated arguments about conflicting ideas. However, believers who are drawn together into community by their shared belief in Christ are also called to that degree of mutual respect such that "two distinct opinions can still praise God with one voice!" (Eugene H. Maly).

When differences are respected rather than rejected, and when dissenting opinions are openly examined rather than held suspect, then the resulting blend of pluralistic views makes their union all the more complete and remarkable. With faith, endurance and courage, a cacophony can become a harmonious symphony.

The prayer for peace, joy and abounding hope with which Paul concludes his call to unity (Romans 15:13) continues to speak to the needs and desires of modern believers. Paul's unflappable optimism and his confidence in the future of the Roman community offer encouragement to those who seek to share their lives and their futures with one another. Marital union becomes possible when each partner in the relationship looks beyond himself/herself to value and respect the distinctiveness of the other. When the burdens of the other become my own, and when the interests of the other outweigh my own in importance, then shall two voices be heard as one.

You are not your own

The decade of the 60s in this country has been characterized as a period of sexual revolution when centuries-old sexual mores and values were cast off in the name of freedom and personal expression. However, with the unrelenting onset of the AIDS epidemic in the 80s, the sexual habits of the U.S. and the world began to change. Casual sex, previously touted as a mark of the liberated person, has been replaced by "safe sex" and, in some cases, by abstinence. Public service announcements geared toward an increasingly younger audience warn against behaviors which may place the individual at risk of contracting this dreaded and fatal illness. In his first letter to the Christians at Corinth, Paul also warned against too casual an attitude toward sexuality; however, fear of sickness and death was not a factor in his argument.

Like others in the ancient Near Eastern world who were influenced by a dualistic gnostic philosophy, the Corinthians had little regard for the human body. They believed that, because God permitted the demise of the body in death, he therefore concurred with their assessment (Jerome Murphy-O'Connor). Consequently, since bodily actions were thought to have no moral value, any and every corporeal activity was permitted, even in excess. "Every sin which a man commits is outside the body" (v. 18) was a popular Corinthian slogan which negated responsibility for sins involving bodily appetites. The Corinthians accepted as sinful only those acts associated with *motive* and *intention*. Paul insisted that the misuse of sex is a sin against one's very self.

In rejecting the Corinthian view about the body, Paul focused attention on the fact of Jesus' resurrection. The Son of God became incarnate and, through his bodily existence, reconciled humanity with God. Now raised from death by God, Jesus in his resurrection underscores the value and dignity of the body. Those who are by faith members of Christ's body which is the church will enjoy a similar victory over sin and death.

When Paul challenged the Corinthians to live moral, holy lives, he appealed not to their fear of sickness or death but to their sense of honor. Redeemed at great cost, viz., the death of Jesus on the cross, the Corinthians had been blessed by God with a share in the life which Jesus shared with the Father. They were recipients of the gift of the Spirit and, by virtue of that gift, their bodies (communally and individually) were to be revered as temples. To behave in a lewd manner was understood by Paul as a desecration of the body which had been made holy by the very presence of God. Paul's statement, "You are not your own," undercut the self-sufficiency of those who engaged in sexual license. For Paul, those redeemed by the blood of Christ no longer belong to sin or to death or even to their own desires; the redeemed belong to God and their bodies are deserving of only the most careful and reverent stewardship.

To those whose behavior devalued, ignored and/or abused the body, Paul proclaimed, "Glorify God in your body." For us human beings who exercise our existence and explore our world through our bodies and whose most intimate relationships are sealed and celebrated through bodily expression, Paul's advice is a constant reminder of our grace and dignity.

Above all, love

*I*n Paul's day, Corinth was a busy seaport metropolis strategically located at the juncture of the east-west and north-south trade routes that spanned the Roman empire. The capital of the Roman province of Achaia, Corinth was home to a mixed population of Romans, Greeks and Jews. Retired Roman soldiers rubbed shoulders with international merchants; freed persons and slaves, philosophers and artists, athletes (Corinth hosted the Isthmian games), ascetics and atheists, all contributed to the pluralism of ideas and influences that was Corinth.

During his stay in Corinth, Paul was successful in establishing an enthusiastic Christian community which met and celebrated the faith in the city's several house churches. Paul maintained contact with the Corinthian church through letters and messengers; from his letters, it is clear that the community was a factious one.

Disputes arose over several issues. Believers were at odds over their preference for certain preachers of the good news (1 Corinthians 1:10-17). Others disagreed about how to handle the public scandal of an incestuous relationship (1 Corinthians 5:1-13). Ascetics reacted to the practices of libertines; conservatives and liberals argued about the consuming of meat that had been sacrificed to idols (1 Corinthians 8-9). The value of certain spiritual gifts was debated (1 Corinthians 12-14) and some Christians made use of the civil courts to subject others to litigation (1 Corinthians 6:1-11). Unfortunately, these disagreements found their way to the eucharistic table and the celebration of love and unity became a sham (1 Corinthians 11:17-34).

Aware of all of these difficulties, Paul called the believers in Corinth to a reassessment of themselves and the commitment to Christ which they shared. "Set your heart on the greater gifts," he implored as he attempted to focus the various factions of the Corinthian church on the one factor that outweighed and surpassed all other concerns: love.

Paul understood that the "love of God which has been poured out into our hearts through the Holy Spirit" (Romans 5:5) is the source and substance which constitutes Christian identity. For this reason, he explained, "if I have not love, I am nothing." The word for "nothing" in Greek connotes more than uselessness; it means to be non-existent. Therefore, even the most spiritually gifted community is unauthentic and meaningless without love.

In 1 Corinthians 13:1-3, Paul cites several of the more admired and coveted spiritual gifts, e.g., tongues, prophecy, knowledge, faith, and underscores the emptiness of these exercises if they are not informed and motivated by love. Even almsgiving to the extreme and death by torture have no value if not supported and sustained by love.

Then Paul paints for his readers a verbal portrait of love, composed of 15 characteristics. Rather than define love as an abstract entity, Paul conveys the essence of love by describing what it does or does not do. Each quality of love named by Paul represents an aspect of human interaction which can make or break a relationship. Each quality challenges the individual to be, as Jesus was, a person for the other and for others.

Each quality challenges the believer to relinquish a "Ptolemaic" view of life, viz., that the world revolves around me, and to embrace the "Copernican" view that I and all those with whom I live revolve around and depend upon the "Son" as our center. The altruism demanded by love places others, their needs and interests first, and promotes healthy, harmonious and holy relationships.

Eyebrow to eyebrow

*O*ne of the so-called disputed or deutero-Pauline letters, Ephesians nevertheless reflects Paul's awareness of Christ and the church and may be the work of a Pauline disciple intent upon accommodating his mentor's insights for a new generation of believers (ca. 80s CE). The author's primary thesis in the letter is that God has "made known to us in all wisdom and insight the mystery of his will, according to his purpose which he set forth in Christ as a plan for the fullness of time, to unite all things in him, things in heaven and things on earth" (Ephesians 1:9-10).

According to the letter's author, Christ was the great reconciler who united humanity with God and all of humankind with one another; the church which is the body of Christ is to continue the work of its head. In other words, christology dictates ecclesiology.

For those (like myself) with a penchant for etymologies, the term "reconciliation" is a veritable treasure trove of delights! In breaking down the word into its basic components, we have the prefix "re-" from the Latin "again" while "-con-" comes from the Latin "with" or "together." From the Latin also comes "-cilia-" meaning "hairs" or "hair-like projections." If we think of those hairs in terms of eyebrows or eyelashes, then "reconciliation" can mean a process of "coming eyebrow to eyebrow together again" with God!

Those who meet one another eyebrow to eyebrow are those who have overcome their differences and scaled what seemed to be insurmountable obstacles in order to see eye to eye. Believers in Jesus Christ and in the saving power of his cross realize that this nearness to God (reconciliation) has been accomplished through him. Moreover, because of the inherent unity of Christ and the church, it devolves upon the church to continue the process of bringing all peoples eyebrow to eyebrow together again with one another in Christ, and with Christ to the Father.

Although he did not speak in terms of eyebrows, the author of Ephesians underscored the seven pillars of Christian unity (one body, one Spirit, one hope, one Lord, one faith, one baptism, one God and Father) and called his readers to live lives worthy of the gift of unity which was Christ's legacy to them. Some biblical scholars have suggested that the seven "one" statements were incorporated into the rite of baptism as liturgical shouts of joy.

Aware that the Christian's vocation of bringing reconciliation among his/her contemporaries is no mean feat, the Ephesians" author cited four virtues which catalyzed the process: (1) Humility (Greek *tapeinophrosune*) is the basic sense of self-worth and reverence for others which comes from knowledge of Christ and knowledge of self before Christ. The humble person has a "down-to-earth, feet-on-the-ground" (*humus*) attitude which promotes wholesome, holy relationships. (2) Gentleness (Greek *praotes*) is a term used to describe an animal that has been housebroken or domesticated. The gentle believer has been domesticated or brought into the household of the faith and will spend all his/her energies and efforts in the service of Christ and the church. (3) Patient bearing with one another (Greek *makrothumia*) describes that attitude which refuses to retaliate and which bears even insult without bitterness. (4) Love (Greek *agapé*) has been aptly described by William Barclay as an "unconquerable benevolence" which flows not from the *emotions* but the *will* of the believer.

At first glance, this catalog of virtues may appear to be an impossible challenge, but the author of Ephesians had previously assured his readers that they would be "strengthened with power through the Spirit," and that they had been "blessed in Christ with every spiritual blessing" (Ephesians 3:16, 1:3).

For those who enter the intimate community of marriage, these virtues make possible the sometimes seemingly impossibility of a lifelong commitment. Humility, gentleness, patience and love make it possible for two people to engage in that daily process of reconciliation (eyebrow to eyebrow) which creates true oneness and peace.

Code of conduct

*I*n recent decades, some biblical scholars have expanded their field of study to include an exploration of the social structures and conventions within which the scriptures developed. One such expert in this field of social science methodology, Derek Tidball, has identified the household unit as the primary structure of the Roman empire. Households consisted of a number of families, friends, dependents and slaves who were bound together under the authority of the senior male member of the principal family. Each of these households had certain rules, a household code which specified the responsibilities and rights of each member and protected the harmonious ordering of all household activities. Tidball has also noted that households usually adopted common religious beliefs and practices, and that early Christianity was well served by the vitality and solidarity of the sociological model of the converted household.

This excerpt from the letter to the Ephesians presumes the existence of the household unit as the essential structure of the growing Christian community with the household code as its guiding norm. Part of a longer series of instructions on how "to live in a manner worthy of the call you have received" (Ephesians 4:1), these imperatives are motivated not simply by the need for an ordered and harmonious household but by love and reverence for Christ. Challenging his readers to "follow the way of love" (Ephesians 5:2), the Ephesians' author elaborated the manner in which that love should be reflected in all the household's interpersonal relationships. Ordinarily, the head of the household exercised an unquestioned authority over all others simply by virtue of his position in the family hierarchy, but Christian households were called to a higher standard, viz., the self-giving and sacrificial love of Christ (v. 2, "he gave himself for us").

Viewed within the context of that great love, the submission of wives to their husbands and the unreserved love of husbands for their wives is raised to a new level and reaches beyond societal mores to an ecclesial and christological dimension. As Reginald Fuller has pointed out, the author's doctrine of the church and of Christ's relationship to the church is not built up *from below,* i.e., from a natural understanding of marriage; rather, he has *raised to a new level* the understanding of marriage and set it within the context of the mystical union of Christ and the church. By associating the institution of marriage with the divine intention for creation (Ephesians 5:31 = Genesis 2:24) rather than with the human social order, the author of Ephesians sublimated the spousal relationship that was so denigrated by many of his contemporaries. In his commentary on Ephesians, William Barclay described this Christian view of marriage as one which probably seemed revolutionary in its societal context. The triplet of cultures that dominated most of the Roman empire (Roman, Greek and Jewish) held women in low esteem. Although marriage was considered an ideal, it had been demeaned and weakened by the ease with which divorces were granted and partners were changed. Calling his contemporaries to a loving and caring reverence for the marital relationship, the Christian author of Ephesians did much to elevate the position of wives and mothers in his society.

Although many today regard this text from Ephesians as sexist and limited by the paternalistic culture within which it originated, nevertheless these exhortations remain a challenge to anyone who would enter into the sacred mystery of marriage. Notice the fact that the author compares the commitment of marriage to the commitment of Christ on behalf of humanity. By the gift of himself, Christ brought purification, nourishment and life to the church. Those who would engage in marriage should be prepared to give of themselves, each to the other, in a similar manner.

Joyful ideals

When Paul founded the Christian community in Philippi, he was well aware of its historic and political importance. Philippi was the site of the last battle of the republicans of Rome. There Antony and Octavian (the future Augustus) defeated Cassius and Brutus in 42 BCE. Sixteen centuries later, the great bard of Avon, William Shakespeare, dramatized this event and quite accurately described the topography of Philippi in his play, *Julius Caesar* (act V, scene i).

Because the Philippians had supported his cause, Octavian Augustus later made the city a Roman colony and endowed its inhabitants with the rights of citizenship in the empire. Eventually, Philippi became home to a large population of retired Roman soldiers and their families.

In their commentary on the great apostle and his letters, W. J. Conybeare and J. S. Howson remarked that Paul had come to Philippi to wage an even greater battle (than Antony and Octavian did against Brutus and Cassius) and to further the cause of a kingdom more lasting than Rome. Moreover, Paul had come as an emissary of one whose gift of peace (Philippians 4:7) far surpassed the imposed and enforced *pax romana*. Elsewhere in his correspondence to Philippi (3:20), Paul reminded the Philippians that they were not simply citizens of the Roman empire but that they had been blessed with citizenship in heaven.

Because of the spiritual privileges they enjoyed in Christ, Paul called the Philippians to a way of life that worthily reflected all they had received. He reminded them to hold fast to what they had "learned, received, heard and seen in him" (v. 9). By using the specific term *paralambanein* ("received"), Paul underscored the fact that his words and work among the Philippians had been authoritative and true. Indeed, as a genuine apostle, he was handing on what he himself had received (1 Corinthians 15:3), viz., the authentic saving truth of the good news.

No doubt, this assertion assured the Philippians who were plagued by those whom Paul called "dogs" and "evil-workers" and "enemies of the cross of Christ" (Philippians 3:2, 18). These false teachers (Judaizers?) traveled in Paul's footsteps, telling his converts that he had diluted the good news for their sake and that they must go through Moses and the Jewish law in order to truly come to Christ. The Philippian believers were also troubled by hostile neighbors who rejected their faith and lifestyle. Internal disputes among community members (Euodia and Syntyche, Philippians 4:2-3) were also a source of tension.

Aware of all that troubled the church in Philippi, Paul (writing from prison) urged them to look beyond the daily grind and to celebrate Christ and his nearness with joy. Rather than worry, they should pray so that they might rise above the strife and pettiness to set their hearts and minds on truth, honor, justice, purity, loveliness, graciousness and excellence (Philippians 4:8). These were Roman Stoic ideals familiar to the Philippians, but they were qualities that would inspire goodness and foster union among those who valued them.

Today, as statisticians bombard us with data concerning marriage and the major causes of conflict and divorce (economic problems, irreconcilable differences, lack of communication, infidelity, sexual incompatibility, etc.), we would do well to remember Paul's counsels concerning the unity which can exist and grow between persons who love one another in the Lord.

The heart's umpire

One of the principles underpinning the four major documents
(or "constitutions") of the Second Vatican Council was a renewed emphasis on the significance of baptism. In propound-
ing the theology of the sacrament and in revising the manner
in which it is to be celebrated, the council fathers stated:
"Through baptism, we are formed in the likeness of Christ. . . .
In this sacred rite, fellowship in Christ's death and resurrection is symbolized and brought about. Incorporated into the
church by baptism, the faithful are reborn as children of God;
they must profess before humankind the faith they have received" (*Lumen gentium* [Dogmatic Constitution on the
Church], nos. 7, 9).

By calling Christians to a deepened awareness of their
baptismal commitment, the church instigated a tidal wave
of growth and grace and renewal that has alternately ebbed
and flowed in the lives of believers for over 30 years. When
the author of the letter to the Colossians became aware of
the fact that certain false ideas (an incipient form of gnosticism) were threatening the integrity of the faith, he also
called his readers to rethink their baptismal commitment.

After establishing the primacy of Christ (Colossians
1:15-20) over all creation and above all other powers (some
in Colossae ascribed to the influence of angel intermediar-
ies, astral powers, etc.), the author of Colossians reminded
his readers that they had died with Christ in baptism and
were alive in him through faith (Colossians 2:12) and were
to live according to that gracious gift of redemption. They
were, in effect, to *die* to all immorality, vice, etc. (Colossians
3:5-9) and *live* the *new life* of love, peace and goodness
which Christ had made possible. This pericope details the
virtues which should characterize the life in Christ of the
baptized believer.

Applying to the predominantly gentile community in Colossae the words which had once solely described Israel ("chosen," "holy," "beloved"—v. 12), the author reminded his readers that, in the economy of salvation brought about by Christ, there is no "most favored nation" status (W. Barclay). Indeed, anything that would cause separation and/or alienation between individuals and/or nations was to be superseded by the peace of Christ. William Barclay has suggested that modern translators would do well to use the literal rendering of v. 15: "Let the peace of Christ be the umpire in your heart." Aware of the inevitable conflicts that arise in community when opinions differ and feelings flare, the Colossians' author focused on the one norm which could heal rifts and restore harmony: Christ's peace. If peace is the arbiter, then love can flourish and, with it, all of its manifestations, e.g., mercy, kindness, forgiveness and mutual service, instruction and correction.

Three times in this short pericope, the believers of Colossae are called to be thankful (vv. 15-17). As Paul Wrightman has noted, "Thankfulness is not an optional or recommended part of the Christian life, but an essential expression of the Christian's transforming and empowering relationship with God." Thankfulness precludes pride and arrogance because it focuses attention on the giver rather than on oneself.

This outward and Christ-centered focus enables the believer to love and to live for others. This altruistic love supports healthy and holy relationships between spouses, among family members and within the community as a whole.

Pilgrims on the way

*I*n the 30 years since the Second Vatican Council, believers have become accustomed to describing the church as "the pilgrim people of God." However, this ecclesial insight, put forth in *Lumen gentium* (Dogmatic Constitution on the Church, chapter VII, nos. 48-51), is actually rooted in a much older document. Writing in the last third of the first Christian century, the anonymous author of Hebrews identified the church with ancient Israel during its years of traveling through the wilderness. Like Israel, the church is a people on the way to a future, heavenly goal. "Having here no lasting city" (Hebrews 13:14), the church is the "wandering people of God." (Ernst Käsemann).

Although this image of the church was based upon a reflection on Jewish tradition, it was also related to the actual situation of the church to which the author addressed his written sermon. "Plainly in need of challenge, and in danger of losing faith and never reaching the promised rest, the church faced the danger of weariness after the hope and enthusiasm of the earliest days had faded—many were tempted to abandon the journey . . . to fall back into Judaism or perhaps simply into conventional lifeless piety" (Robert A. Spivey, D. Moody Smith, Jr.).

The author of Hebrews intended that his readers see Christ and the church as the definitive fruit and full flower of Judaism. All that had been written in Jewish tradition pointed to Jesus and validated his existence. Similar to the theologies preached by the Hellenist Christians (Acts 7) and the Johannine community, the message of Hebrews underscored Jesus as the replacement of the Jewish cult, its temple, clergy and sacrificial system. Believers in Jesus' saving work were called to find their journey's end in him, and with him to celebrate his once-for-all saving sacrifice and his unique and eternal priesthood.

This pericope is part of the sermon's final chapter and consists mainly of practical instructions; nevertheless, it is logically connected to the theological argument put forth in the 12 preceding chapters. Because of their faith in Jesus who is "the same yesterday, today and forever" (Hebrews 13:8), believers are to live accordingly: *in* the world but not defined or determined by its standards and values. Christians are to persevere in mutual love and hospitality. The prisoners (v. 3) whom they were called to support were probably fellow believers, incarcerated for reasons of faith, debt or poverty. In *The Apology,* Tertullian wrote: "If there happens to be anyone in the mines, or banished to the islands, or shut up in prisons for nothing but their fidelity to the cause of God's church, they become the nurslings of their confession."

Marriage was to be honored as a relationship which formed families and fostered the environment in which the young grow up in the rich heritage of the faith.

Rather than spend their energies on capitalism and its gains, Christians—who are merely sojourners in this world— are to value all things in terms of those *lasting gifts* which alone give life, purpose and meaning. The promise, "I will never forsake or abandon you" (based on Deuteronomy 31:6 and Joshua 1:5) is a *gift* of presence which God realized for his people in the person and mission of Jesus Christ. This gift guides and sustains the pilgrim people on its journey home.

When married persons share their lives with one another as pilgrims on the way, their values will be truer, their investments wiser, their petty differences fewer. Their long term plans and short term goals will benefit from a perspective which rises above daily concerns to focus on lasting riches.

God is love

When Jesus instructed his contemporaries in the cost of discipleship, he left no doubt as to the struggle his committed followers would face: "Do not think that I have come to bring peace upon the earth. I have come to bring not peace but the sword. For I have come to set a man against his father, a daughter against her mother . . . and one's enemies will be those of his household" (Matthew 10:34-36). In the decade following the resurrection, as more and more believers accepted the challenge of the gospel and became disciples, the struggle of which Jesus had spoken became a poignant and personal reality in many lives.

Very often, whole households were converted to Christ and supported one another in living out their baptismal commitment. But frequently, as in the situation reflected in this pericope, only one or a few members of a household became Christian. Their commitment to Christ was seen as a threat to household unity and harmony, and these believers were mistreated and harassed by the societies in which they lived.

Aware of the conflict faced by his readers in Asia Minor, the author of 1 Peter advised those who were being "spoken of as evildoers" (! Peter 2:12), "insulted" (3:9) and "vilified" (4:4) to give their enemies no cause for contempt. As "aliens and sojourners" (2:11), believers should conduct themselves as worthy and responsible citizens, honoring all, even the king (2:12-17). Like their contemporaries, Christians were to remain faithful to those domestic codes and rules which secured order and harmony among the household members. However, the believers' motivation for maintaining the household code was distinct from their pagan contemporaries because it was rooted in the baptismal call to life in Christ (1 Peter 1:3-25).

In keeping with the societal mores of the day, women were to obey their husbands. However, the author of 1 Peter called women to live their role as wife and mother so admirably and with such devotion as to evangelize their husbands in the process. By the quality of their lives and the integrity of their character, the so-called "weaker sex" could preach the good news of salvation.

Husbands, for their part, were called to treat their wives with consideration and respect. In the ancient world, women were regarded as property, owned first by their fathers and then by their husbands. Regardless of how these ideas may tweak the 20th-century feminist perspective, the author of 1 Peter actually advanced the cause of women in his society by exhorting men to treat women as persons deserving of reverence. In commenting on this pericope, Luke Timothy Johnson advises us that it is "not a divinely inspired blueprint for the ideal social order or Christian family structure, but the best available moral teaching applied to the real world of that age."

Not to be overlooked is the author's reminder that women and men are joint heirs of the gracious gift of life (3:7). Their partnership in the economy of salvation helps to form the familial matrix in which children can grow up in the heritage of the faith.

Moreover, the author of 1 Peter also counseled his readers that a prayerful relationship with God is not possible unless it is supported by and reflected in a healthy and holy relationship with one's spouse (3:7). Only when the Christian household is characterized by mutual love, honor and support will its members be empowered to fend off evil and to answer insults with a blessing (3:8-9).

Love in deed and truth

Over two centuries ago, the founders of this nation labored together to establish a political framework that would enable their contemporaries and future generations to grow and develop. The Declaration of Independence, the Constitution and the Bill of Rights are the foundation blocks of our democracy as well as the matrix within which a variety of diverse political visions have developed. Conservatives, liberals, the "far left" and the "far right," Republicans, Democrats, Independents and Socialists—all lay claim to the same roots of government. Frequently, these various and sundry ideologies clash as each claims its own interpretation and application of the principles of government to be correct. In a sense, this is similar to the situation that existed within the Johannine community.

Rooted in the good news of Jesus as recorded in the fourth gospel, the community grew and developed within the rich framework of Johannine theology. By the end of the first Christian century, however, conflicting understandings of the gospel became a source of tension within the community. The struggle was exacerbated by the fact that the two opposing groups each claimed to be the true heir and orthodox interpreter of the gospel tradition. One group comprised the author of 1 John and his adherents; eventually, this group blended with the rest of the church catholic. The other group seceded from the community and gradually melded with a variety of heretical gnostic and/or docetic groups. This particular pericope is a plea for unity that the author of 1 John made to the so-called secessionists.

Whereas the dissidents denied the true humanity of Jesus and claimed to possess eternal life by virtue of knowing God, they were indifferent to ethical behavior, believing it to have no salvific value. On the other hand, the author of 1 John and his adherents underscored the essence of Christian living as a combination of *belief* in Jesus Christ and *love* for one another (1 John 3:23). As Raymond E. Brown has explained, belief in Jesus is actually faith in God whose Son he is; this belief is made possible only by the "vertical" action of God who sent his Son. Correspondingly, the believers' love for one another is a "horizontal" but essential continuation of the "vertical" love God has shown. Therefore, belief and love are not two distinct virtues but two dimensions of the same expression of the Christian life (John 13:34-36, 15:12-17).

By exhorting his contemporaries to "love in deed and in truth and not merely talk about it" (1 John 3:18), the author of 1 John reminded them (and us) of the essential integrity of Christian faith. Without belief in God, even the most generous deeds are mere ethical humanism; informed by belief, however, the believer's loving goodness toward another is an eloquent witness to the truth of Christ. Moreover, the secessionists, who claimed to have special knowledge of God and therefore to live in his truth, were called to translate that knowledge into care, love and service for others.

Where belief and love form the linchpins of Christian living, there the Spirit of God remains (1 John 3:24). For the author of 1 John, this was the ultimate test of authenticity. Those who were the genuine adherents of the Johannine gospel would be the true heirs of the Spirit promised therein (John 14:16-17, 26; 16:13). Only the legitimate heirs of the Spirit would be empowered with the capacity for *belief* and for *love*.

*F*or two people desirous of celebrating their love for one another in the sacrament of marriage, the advice of 1 John remains a timely challenge. If love is to endure, the words, "I love you," must be translated into the language of daily deeds and truthfulness (1 John 3:18). Moreover, if love is to last, it must be founded on a shared belief in God. Those who share both belief and love will also share in the power of the indwelling Spirit.

God is love

If nothing else in praise of love was said in the rest of the epistle, nay in the rest of scripture, and we had heard from the mouth of the Spirit of God only that one statement, "God is love," we would not have to look for anything else.

With this statement, St. Augustine affirmed his conviction that the author of 1 John had succeeded in distilling the good news into one powerful proclamation, "God is love" (1 John 4:8).

As Raymond E. Brown has explained, "God is love" is a *theological* formula which contrasts God's posture toward humanity with that of the world which is characterized by hatred (1 John 3:13). Moreover, "God is love" is a *christological* formula in the same way that "God is light" (1 John 1:5) and "God is Spirit" (John 4:24) are christological statements. Just as it is only through Jesus the Christ that believers know God as Spirit (John 7:39) and as light (John 8:12), so too, it is only because of and through Jesus that we can know God as love. As the writer of 1 John points out, the definitive revelation of God's love is the incarnation (1 John 4:9) and the redeeming death of Jesus (1 John 4:10, 1 John 3:16). In this, the author reiterates the tradition preserved in the Johannine gospel (John 3:16-17).

In addition to being a *theological* and *christological* statement, "God is love" is also a *moral imperative* for all who profess belief in God because it devolves upon Christians to live out the implications of this reality in the words and works that shape their daily lives.

Aimed at those inheritors of the Johannine tradition (see the commentary on 1 John 3:18-24, pages 95-96, for an explanation of the Johannine community) who professed to have special, esoteric knowledge of God and/or a unique intuition or vision of God but who placed no salvific value on moral behavior, the message of 1 John is clear: Only those who love one another know God.

The author of 1 John also understood the mutual love among believers as an integral part of God's saving plan and an aspect of *revelation*. Just as the love of God became a flesh and blood reality, "revealed in our midst" in Jesus, so must love become incarnate in the lives of Christians. R. Brown describes this continuing revelation of love as the Johannine chain of life-giving: Jesus has life from the Father and the believer has life from Jesus (John 5:26, 6:57; 1 John 5:11-12). Therefore, the way in which the believer lives and the quality of his/her love is a source of life for others.

The initiator of this chain of love and life-giving is, of course, God: "Love then consists in this: not that we have loved God but that he has loved us" (1 John 4:10). If we respond to this loving initiative by loving God and one another, then God's "love is brought to perfection in us" (1 John 4:12). Obviously, the Johannine author is not implying that there is any lack or fault in God's love. Perfection (Greek *teleioun*) means that a process has achieved its goal or has accomplished its intended purpose.

The author of 1 John implores us to acknowledge that the mutual love of believers for one another began with the very essence of God (as love) and became enfleshed in time and space in Jesus. If Christian spouses understand their love as a continuing witness to the presence of God and as a source of revelation and life and love, then their marriage becomes a valuable part of the creative and redemptive process of salvation.

The bridal gown

Weddings were grand and festive occasion in the ancient world. Among the Jews, the ceremony began with the formal writing of the marriage contract. Once the terms of the contract had been agreed to and confirmed by the bride's father and future husband, the nuptial party processed from the bride's family home to her husband's home. Once arrived, the couple was considered legally married and the feasting began.

Unlike modern couples who go off alone to celebrate their union on a honeymoon trip, ancient couples remained at home. With friends, relatives and neighbors, with music, dancing, good food and wine, the newlyweds hosted a week-long party. For many, this was the biggest and best celebration of their lives. It is not surprising, therefore, that marriage and the feasting that accompanied it proved an apt symbol for the joyful union of God and his people.

In the Jewish scriptures, the marital relationship between a man and a woman became a metaphor for the covenantal union of Yahweh and Israel (Hosea 2:16-22; Isaiah 54:5-6, 62:5; Ezekiel 16:6-14). It followed logically that Israel's idolatry and apostasy were likened to the behavior of an adulterous wife (Hosea 2:4-15, Ezekiel 16:15-63). When Israel expressed its hopes for the long awaited messiah, all the joy and abundance of the marriage feast lent themselves to the image of the messianic banquet (Isaiah 25:6). These images, rooted in Jewish tradition, are also expressed in the Christian scriptures (Matthew 22:2, 10, 11; Mark 2:19, John 3:29, 2 Corinthians 11:2, Ephesians 5:21-33).

In this excerpt from the book of Revelation, the seer John understood the marriage motif to denote "the intimate and indissoluble communion of Christ with the community which he had purchased with his own blood" (R. H. Charles). Part of a song of victory (Revelation 19:1-10) occasioned by the final desolation of Babylon, viz., Rome (Revelation 18:21-24), this vision was intended to encourage the Christians of the late first Christian century to persevere in the faith. Persecuted in the reign of the emperor Domitian (81-96 CE), believers in Christ were exhorted to maintain a "bride-like" fidelity to their covenantal partner, the lamb who is Christ.

The figure of the lamb evoked several images and/or motifs, each of which added a unique facet to the heavenly celebration of salvation. First, the passover lamb whose blood saved Israel from death (Exodus 12:21-23); then, the suffering, silent lamb whose innocent sacrifice healed our sins (Isaiah 52:13—53:12); and finally, the conquering lamb who will destroy all evil (Revelation 7:17, 17:14). All these themes are embodied in Jesus, the lamb of God who invites the faithful to his feast.

In her commentary on Revelation, Adela Y. Collins draws our attention to the dress of the bride or the faithful believer. Notice that she has been *given* a dress to wear (v. 8a). This statement, says Collins, underscores the fact that salvation is a *gift* from God to his people (see Isaiah 61:10). However, the description of the dress ("the linen dress is the virtuous deeds of God's saints," v. 8b) reminds the believer of his/her responsibility for tending that gift through all the struggles and exigencies of daily life.

When two people commit themselves to Christ and to one another in love, the gift of salvation and the responsibility for tending it together become a source of deeper, fuller union.

Gospel

MATTHEW 5:1-12

The beatitudes

---

*I*n the 1983 pastoral letter, *The Challenge of Peace: God's Promise and Our Response,* the National Conference of Catholic Bishops underscored the need for peace among all nations and lamented the travesty of war. Identifying Jesus as the one whose blood and cross made true peace a reality in the world (Colossians 1:19-20), the bishops cited the Great Sermon as the "program" which challenges believers to be the architects and mediators of that peace for all peoples (*The Challenge of Peace,* no. 45).

Throughout the centuries since Jesus' first advent, the Great Sermon has been variously described as: (1) a pernicious document which represents an impossible ideal (Martin Luther), (2) extreme demands which prompt the believer to "exert himself/herself seriously in an attempt to attain (at least) part of them" (Joachim Jeremias), (3) an "interim ethic" or a "last ditch" effort at heroic moral conversion to prepare for Jesus' second advent (Johannes Weiss).

While each of these proposals contains some element of truth with regard to the Great Sermon, none is completely accurate. In a word, the Great Sermon (and, specifically, the beatitudes) represents the call of Jesus to his followers to live every aspect of their lives as citizens of the kingdom he came to proclaim. The kingdom or saving reign of God over his people is characterized by mercy, peace, love, forgiveness, mutual caring and fierce opposition to all that detracts from God-given human dignity, viz., injustice, evil and abuse of the downtrodden.

The values of the kingdom or the reign of God were as counter-cultural in Jesus' day as they are today. Jesus' words challenged and continue to challenge believers to live contrary to the status quo, to "buck" the system which preaches the advancement of the individual, his/her desires and dreams at all costs. But as revolutionary as Jesus' ideas might seem, they had roots in Jewish tradition.

The poor ones or *anawim* were those who were without material possessions and were thereby thought to be accursed by God; however, their confidence and reliance on God made them the heirs of the promises of salvation (Isaiah 61:1f = Luke 4:18f; Zephaniah 2:3). Both Matthew and the Essenes of the Qumran community (1QM14, 7) added the modifier, "in spirit," to extend the beatitude beyond the materially needy to embrace persons of every social class who would depend completely on God.

Jesus' blessings of the mournful, the meek and the clean of heart are also reflected in the Jewish scriptures (Isaiah 61:2, Psalm 37:11, Psalm 24:4). However, while the Old Testament texts referred to these groups in terms of future promises, Jesus became the fulfiller of those promises in his person and in his mission.

Perhaps the first step in living the noble ethic put forth in the beatitudes is to take the teaching seriously. The second is to realize that the believer is not alone in facing the daily and often unpopular challenge of Christian living. By his own example and the gift of his Spirit, Jesus empowers and supports those who would hear his words and keep them.

When two people marry, their love for one another creates a home for future believers; the privilege and responsibility of sharing the faith is primarily theirs. Theirs also is the challenge of providing a place where Christian values are taught and nurtured as real possibilities and where young people can develop the strengths and talents required to live the gospel in the world.

In the words of the American Catholic bishops: "Parents, your role is unsurpassed by any other; the foundation of society is the family. . . . Children hear the gospel message first from your lips. Parents who consciously discuss issues of justice in the home and who strive to help children solve conflicts through non-violent methods enable their children to grow up as peacemakers" (The Challenge of Peace, *no. 306).*

Light and salt

Nil utilius sole et sale ("There is nothing more useful than sunlight and salt").

With these words, the ancient Roman scholar Pliny the Elder (23-79 CE) affirmed the elemental significance of Jesus' challenge to his disciples: "You are the salt of the earth . . . you are the light of the world" (*Natural History*, 31:102; Matthew 5:13a, 14a).

Whereas the ancient Greeks regarded salt as divine (*theion*), the Romans believed it to be the purest of all things and the greatest gift of the gods to humankind. Formed by the mysterious cooperation of the sun and the sea, salt was used as a preservative, enabling the extended storage of meats and fish. Newborn babies were rubbed with salt because it was believed to strengthen and toughen them against the elements. Used extensively as a seasoning, salt imparted taste to an otherwise bland diet. Many ancient peoples (including the Israelites) formed covenants of friendship by sharing salt with one another (Numbers 18:19, 2 Chronicles 13:5). Among the Israelites, sacrifices to Yahweh were considered more pleasing if accompanied by an offering of salt.

When Jesus identified his followers in terms of salt, all of these characteristic qualities were implied. Just as salt preserved food, so Jesus' disciples are to preserve or save the people among whom they live and labor. Just as salt imparted taste and strength, so the disciples are to spend themselves in building up the human community with an enthusiastic zest for life and for giving. And just as salt was used to seal the bonds of covenants and to offer gifts to God, so Jesus' disciples are to be the catalysts of good relationships in society as well as between God and his people.

No less important than salt, light was associated with life, goodness, joy and glory. Cicero (106-43 BCE), the Roman statesman, lawyer and writer, applauded Rome as "light to the whole world" (*hanc urbem, lucem orbis terrarum atque ar-*

cem omnium gentium; In Catalinam **IV**, vi, 11). Among the Israelites, the Torah (the law), the scribes, Jerusalem and the rabbis were variously described as being light for Israel and for the world. A quality ascribed in Jewish tradition to God and to his word (Exodus 24:10; Psalm 104:2, 19:8, 27:1, 119:130), the prerogative of being light was applied by Jesus to those who believed in him (John 1:1-18, Matthew 4:12-17; Luke 1:79, 2:32). In his words and works, Jesus superseded the law, Jerusalem, the scribes and the rabbis as the true and eternal light made visible in the world.

The fact that Jesus charged his disciples with being light indicated that he intended his followers to share in his mission of illuminating and guiding the world on its path to the Father.

Significantly, Jesus' dual challenge to be both salt and light for the world, which was probably circulated as two originally independent sayings (notice their context in other gospels), has been placed at the conclusion of the beatitudes. As John Meier has noted, "Those persecuted by the world, as in Matthew 5:1-12, are nevertheless the world's salvation." They exist and are for the world as necessary as salt and light. Therefore, they may not remain withdrawn or hidden but their actions must be a visible and vital aspect of life in the world.

Christian couples and their families can make an invaluable contribution to the societies in which they live by taking Jesus' words to heart. First, Christian spouses are called to be both salt and light for one another; and then, together they can co-operate to be both salt and light for their families and for the world.

The two foundations

At one time or another, all of us have filled out a questionnaire or responded to a survey that requested certain statistical information from us. In addition to sex, race, age, marital status, political persuasion, etc., there may have been an item regarding religious preference. But, as each of us knows, the mere fact that a person identifies as a Christian, Jew or Moslem is not an accurate indication of spiritual integrity. Indeed, the only reliable measure of a person's true religious identity is the degree to which professed faith affects the quality of daily thoughts, words, actions and ethical choices. This is the premise that underlies this pericope excerpted from Matthew's gospel.

Part of the conclusion of the Great Sermon, this reading constitutes the last in a series of antithetical parallelisms woven throughout the sermon. In this particular parallelism (the two foundations), the contrast is drawn between false and true disciples. Whereas any follower of Jesus can call upon him, "Lord, Lord," it is only the *true* disciple who translates the implications of that relationship into lived faith.

According to Matthew, the true and sincere disciple is the one who *says* to Jesus, "Lord, Lord," and also *does* the will of the Father (v. 21). Similarly, the true disciple is the one who *listens* to the will of the Father as it is revealed in the words of Jesus and *acts* upon it (v. 24). The connection between saying and doing or hearing and doing is absolutely necessary. As John Meier has pointed out, the *split* between saying and doing or hearing and doing—i.e., hypocrisy—is the essential sin of so-called religious people. Elsewhere in the gospel, the scribes and Pharisees are so accused (Matthew 23:3-5).

In Greek, the verb "to do" (*poieo*) has the additional meaning "to bear fruit." "By their fruits you shall know them" is a challenge issued earlier in the Great Sermon (Matthew 7:20).

Those who say-but-do-not-do or who hear-but-do-not-do have a mere nominal association with Christ. These can be compared to those who build their houses on a shaky foundation. When difficulties arise, the house falls . . . the relationship evaporates . . . the name "Christian" is a lie. But, like the house built upon a firm foundation, those will endure whose relationship with Christ includes both saying and doing as well as hearing and doing.

The evangelist may have had in mind the proverb preserved in the rich heritage of Jewish literature: "When the tempest passes, the wicked person is no more, but the just person is established forever" (Proverbs 10:25). Or he may have wanted to remind his readers of the rabbinical image of the man learned in the law whose "house" (life) was considered sturdy or shoddy depending upon the presence or absence of his good deeds.

In his commentary on Matthew's gospel, William Barclay summed up the message of this short reading and the challenge of Jesus' aspiring disciples in these words: "Knowledge must become action; theory must become practice; theology must become life."

On their wedding day, two people stand before God, family and friends to hear *the terms. challenges and blessings that will constitute their mutual commitment; on that day they* say *the words that promise enduring love and fidelity. But in order for their marriage to be happy and true, all that they have been* hearing *and* saying *must become a matter of* doing *each day of their life together. It is significant that the words with which each of the married partners pledges his/her love are: "I do."*

Grounds for marriage

*T*he 1993 edition of the *World Almanac and Book of Facts* lists the following as grounds given for divorce between American couples: cruelty, adultery, desertion, insanity, impotence, bigamy, alcoholism, drug addiction, felony conviction and/or imprisonment. In some states, the vague term, "irreconcilable differences," is sufficient to permit the dissolution of a marriage. When the Pharisees approached Jesus with the question, "May a man divorce his wife for *any reason whatsoever?*", they probably wished to draw him into an arena of argument that was as controversial in the 30s CE as it continues to be today. No doubt, the Pharisees were already familiar with the radical nature of Jesus' teaching about marriage and divorce (Matthew 5:31-32; see above, pages 00-00) and wished to question him further.

Among the Israelites, marriage was regarded as a sacred duty. Only those wishing to devote their lives to the study of the Torah were exempt from married life and family responsibilities. According to the rabbis, he who had no children "slew his own posterity" and "lessened the image of God upon earth. . . . When husband and wife are worthy, the glory of God is with them" (William Barclay).

The Hebrew term for marriage is *kiddushin* which means "sanctification" or "consecration." A term usually used to describe people or objects dedicated to God as his exclusive possession, *kiddushin* when applied to the marital relationship implies that each partner surrenders him/herself to the other wholly and exclusively. This is the ideal, but the exigencies of everyday life coupled with human frailty cause many to seek lesser alternatives.

Among Jesus' contemporaries, reasons or grounds for divorce were many and varied, as different rabbis gave their particular interpretations of Deuteronomy 24:1 ("When a man, after marrying a woman and having relations with her, is later displeased with her because he finds in her something indecent . . . he writes out a bill of divorce . . . thus dismissing her from his house"). Everything hung on what might *displease* and what was *something indecent.*

The conservative school of Rabbi Shammai held that "something indecent" referred solely to adultery, whereas the more liberal Rabbi Hillel permitted divorce if a wife: (1) wore her hair unbound and uncovered in public, (2) spoke to men in public, (3) spoke disrespectfully of her parents-in-law in her husband's presence, (4) shouted loud enough to be heard in the next house, (5) over-salted her husband's dinner. Rabbi Akiba taught that a man should be free to divorce if he found someone whom he liked more or whom he found prettier than his wife!

Rather than allow himself to become entangled in this web of controversy, Jesus referred his questioners to the origin and purpose of marriage as stated in Genesis 1:27 and 2:24. Calling the Mosaic ordinance (Deuteronomy 24:1) which permitted divorce a concession to human weakness rather than a law (Matthew 19:7-8), Jesus reaffirmed the permanence and indissolubility of the marriage relationship.

As Benedict Viviano has explained, Jesus' intention was "not to cause pain but to set out a clear and high ideal of human relations, a vision of marriage as a covenant of personal love between spouses which reflects the covenant relationship of God and his people. Unfortunately, this vision does not always fit the vagaries of the human heart (Jeremiah 17:9)."

In its attempts to deal with the tragedy of divorce and its effects upon society, the church recommends extensive premarital preparation. Those who would unite themselves to one another in Christ become an invaluable witness for the rest of society. "Marriage is not just a ceremony by which two people are legally bound together. As a sacrament, it is an act of worship, an expression of faith, a sign of the church's unity, a mode of Christ's presence" in the world (Richard P. McBrien).

A why *to live*

During the Second World War, the noted Viennese psychiatrist, educator and author Victor Frankl and his family were imprisoned by the Nazis at Auschwitz. During three horrific years in what can only be described as bestial conditions, Frankl endured the loss of his father, mother, brother and wife as well as every earthly possession and semblance of human dignity. When asked how he survived such suffering, Frankl quoted Friedrich Nietzsche: "He who has a *why* to live can bear with almost any *how*."

For Frankl, the *why* which sustained him during the years of hunger, loneliness, deprivation and pain was the love he knew for his family and for God. Love gave meaning to his otherwise meaningless existence and fired his will to live. Said Frankl, "The salvation of man is through love and in love . . . love is the ultimate and highest goal to which man can aspire."

When the Pharisaic lawyer came to question Jesus about the law, he was taught a similar lesson. Concerned with the numerous prescriptions of the legal code, the lawyer busied himself with the how aspect of living: *how* to abide by the law, *how* to observe the Sabbath, *how* to conduct his affairs before God and humankind. But Jesus' words challenged him to redirect his energies toward the *why* aspect of human existence and to find the solution to his query in the reality of love.

The question put to Jesus was not unique. Rabbis were frequently requested to summarize the law and/or to determine *that law* upon which all others depended. Often, the questioning of the rabbis and other legal experts followed a discernible structure which consisted of four major elements.

First, the expert was asked to elaborate on the *wisdom* (*hokmah*) of a point of law. Then the questioner attempted to *ridicule* (*boruth*) the belief held by the expert. The third element of the interrogation concerned *fundamental principles for living* (*derek 'eres*); this was the type of question the lawyer put to Jesus. Finally, the rabbi or expert was asked his opinion on a *non-legal teaching* such as a seeming conflict between certain scriptural texts (haggadah). In the series of controversies between Jesus and the Pharisees and Sadducees, Matthew has included all four elements of rabbinic interrogation.

Jesus' response to the lawyer represented a combination on two well-known tenets of the law. The first was drawn from the *Shema' Israel* (Deuteronomy 6:4-5), a prayer every devout Jew prayed daily. Loving God with one's whole heart, soul and mind meant that the totality of the person—intelligence, will, emotions, actions and potential for growth—was to be centered on and motivated by love of God. The second law concerning the love of neighbor was drawn from Leviticus 19:18.

Jesus was not unique in citing these two tenets as the linchpins of the law. Philo of Alexandria (30 BCE-45CE), a Jewish philosopher whose ideas greatly influenced the early church fathers (viz., Clement of Alexandria, Origen and Ambrose) had also offered these as the highest principles of the law (*De Specialis Legibus* 2:63). But Jesus was unique in putting these two tenets on a par with one another. Of the 613 precepts of the law, some were considered "heavy" (or more important) and others were termed "light" (or of lesser importance).

In his statement, "The second is like it" (Matthew 12:39), Jesus explained that the love of God was to be incarnated or translated into the love of neighbor. With this teaching, Jesus made love the canon or measuring stick of true faith, religiosity and morality, and the only acceptable standard of greatness.

Those who marry one another in Jesus' name have the assurance that their selfless love for one another is a reflection of their love for God. It is this love that will sustain and give meaning to their life together. Those "who have a why *to live can bear with almost any* how."

I-thou

When in 1899 Martin Buber, a Jew from Vienna, married Paula Winkler, a Catholic from Munich, the world was experiencing what Buber called "an eclipse of God." Jews were being expelled from Russia, France, Austria and Germany, and no country would accept the thousands who had become refugees. Drawn to one another by mutual ideals and values, Buber and Winkler worked together for the next 60 years "building bridges between Judaism and Christianity in an era that abounded with divisive forces" (Senator Abraham Ribicoff).

Convinced that peace and justice could exist only if people valued and revered the "otherness" of one another, Buber explained that hatred and prejudice result when people treat each other as objects. To do so is to experience and use the other in an "I-it" interchange rather than to truly engage and encounter the other in an "I-thou" relationship.

Although they had come from two different worlds, Paula Winkler and Martin Buber had become one through marriage; each had met the other with reverence as "thou." Buber explained, "Experiencing the other is the essence of love; the turning of the lover to the beloved in his otherness means seeing the other as present for all time. All real living is an encounter or meeting to which a person must bring his/her whole being, his genuine self."

Buber called his wife his "inspiration" and the "touchstone of everything I have done." He also called his marriage the greatest event of his life. Both Martin and Paula were convinced that their union was a God-given gift that required careful and constant tending. Their life together exemplified the essence of the marital relationship as described by Jesus in this Marcan text.

Occasioned by a question asked by some Pharisees concerning the lawfulness of divorce, Jesus' statement is part of a longer narrative (Mark 10:1-12) which defined his teaching on marriage and divorce.

As Daniel Harrington has noted, the question (Mark 10:2, "Is it lawful for a husband to divorce his wife?") was expressed in such a way as to indicate that the questioners knew Jesus' prohibition of divorce conflicted with the prescription detailed in Deuteronomy 24:1-4. Perhaps the questioners wished to draw Jesus into conflict with the much-divorced Herod family. Explaining that the regulations on divorce in Deuteronomy (24:1-4) were a concession due to their "hardness of heart" (Mark 10:5), Jesus cited other scriptural texts (Genesis 1:27, 2:24) which underscored marriage as a divinely intended permanent relationship.

Hardness of heart (Greek: *sklerokardia*) referred to that aspect of the human person which refuses to be taught and turns a deaf ear to the call for integrity and holiness. It is this unyielding and self-centered attitude which looks upon others and upon God as "it" rather than as "thou." This thoroughgoing egoism detracts from the giving of oneself to the other which is the essence of marriage.

On countless occasions, "hardness of heart" was cited as the factor which breached the covenant relationship between Yahweh and Israel. In Mark's gospel, Jesus identified this human failing as a factor which erodes the marital covenant between two persons.

Created male and female by God, the human partners in marriage are thereby intended to value and to complement one another to the extent that they become one flesh. When "I" meets "thou" with reverence and altruism, a new existence begins. The name of this new life is "we."

A new order

Weddings and the banquets that celebrate them have been an honored tradition in human society for millennia. Among Jesus' first century CE contemporaries, weddings were welcomed as an opportunity for joy and festivity. Even those with relatively little financial means did their best to provide family and friends with a memorable celebration, made rich and lavish by oriental hospitality. Rather than go away together for a honeymoon, the newly married couple remained in their home to welcome and entertain their guests in a weeklong open house.

Because of the joy and plenty associated with the wedding feast, this particular event lent itself to descriptions of the messianic era of salvation (see Isaiah 25:6-10, 55:1-13, 62:4-5; Wisdom 9:1-18, Revelation 19:6-21).

When the fourth evangelist undertook the task of telling the good news, he was well aware of Israel's mores, scriptural traditions and messianic expectations. To that end, the Johannine narrative of Jesus' first sign at Cana in Galilee was placed within the context of a wedding feast.

With each of the seven signs in the fourth gospel, something of the person and mission of Jesus is revealed, the Father is glorified and those who witnessed the sign (or who later heard and/or read about it) are challenged to believe. Given this function, the sign at Cana served to reveal Jesus as the messiah and inaugurator of the era of salvation.

Wine was considered a sign of messianic times (Amos 9:13-14, Hosea 14:7, Jeremiah 31:12), and the *abundance* of wine Jesus produced served to underscore his messianic identity. An apocryphal Jewish text which appeared contemporaneously with John's gospel described the age of the messiah in this way: "The earth shall yield its fruit 10,000 fold; each vine shall have 1,000 branches; each branch 1,000 clusters, each cluster 1,000 grapes, each grape 120 gallons of wine!" (2 Baruch 29:5).

Each of the six stone water jars at Cana held two to three measures of water; a measure was equivalent to eight gallons. Therefore, each jar held approximately 20 gallons. The six together would have held about 120 gallons of choice wine, an abundance which signaled the messiah and his era.

In addition to its messianic overtones, and in keeping with the Johannine technique known as replacement theology, the event at Cana proclaimed a new order of salvation. The water in the stone jars was used for the ritual ablutions prescribed by Jewish law. Those who kept these rituals were considered "clean," in accord with the law and holy. By replacing the water with "choice wine," Jesus is revealed as "the one sent by the Father, who is now the only way to the Father. All previous religious institutions, customs and feasts lose their meaning in his presence" (Raymond E. Brown). Whereas upright people had formerly regarded the purification rituals as a means of drawing near to God, the sign at Cana makes it clear that Jesus and his choice wine (viz., the gift of salvation that he will give) will henceforth be the way of holiness and of union with the Father.

Like the feast at Cana, the wedding ritual with which two people initiate their life together marks the beginning of a new order. From *that day onward, the* two *shall share in Christ's gifts of salvation and* draw *near to the* Father together.

Chain reaction

Although his liberal political views resulted in his excommunication from Russia's Orthodox Church, the radical social reformer and author, Leo Tolstoy (1828-1910), was clearly a true advocate of Christianity. "There is," he wrote, "only one task for us: to live in love with our brethren, with all of them." Tolstoy had understood the challenge of this short Johannine text whose brevity belies its comprehensiveness.

An excerpt from the longer vine and branches pericope (John 15:1-17) which explores the relationship shared by Jesus and the Father with humankind, this particular text underscores the reality of love as the essential overture of God toward his people. Moreover, these words convey Jesus' challenge to his followers that the only acceptable response to God's loving overtures is a love for Jesus which finds its full expression in our love for one another.

Although there are several words in Greek for "love," the term which is repeated no less than seven times in these verses is *agapan/agapé*. A "unique love made possible through Jesus," *agapé* is a "spontaneous, unmerited, creative love, opening the way to fellowship with God and flowing from God to the Christian and from the Christian to his neighbor" (Anders Nygren and Raymond E. Brown).

As Raymond E. Brown has explained, a pivotal word in this short text is "as" (*kathos*, v. 9). For John, *kathos* is not only *comparative* but also *causative* or *constitutive,* meaning "inasmuch as." Therefore, says Brown, "the Father's love for Jesus is the basis of the love of Jesus for his disciples, both as to origin and intensity." The Father's love sets up a chain reaction of love, as it were: The Father loves Jesus, Jesus loves the disciples, they are to love one another.

By his use of the aorist tense for the verb "to love" (vv. 9, 10, 12), the Johannine author placed emphasis on the fact that Jesus' love for his own is both present and continuous. By use of the present subjunctive ("love one another," v. 12), the author further explained that the love of Jesus' disciples for one another should also be continuous and lifelong.

In his commentary on this Johannine text, Arthur J. Gossip referred to these verses as "staggering words, not easily credible." Gossip found this description of Jesus' love for his own "breath-taking" and "utterly inexplicable." Nevertheless, this is the very heart of the good news summed up so succinctly by John earlier in his gospel: "For God so loved the world that he gave his only Son" (John 3:16). This is the good news that compels those who hear it to live in love and thereby experience great and abiding *joy* (v. 11). Throughout his gospel, John frequently associated Jesus' saving work with joy and rejoicing (John 3:29, 4:36, 8:56, 11:15, 14:28). Significantly, joy and mutual love were factors which attracted many to the early Christian community.

As a very special type of Christian community, married persons are called upon to attract others to Jesus and to the Father. By their mutual love and its resultant joy, those who have become one in the love of Christ are a living sacrament of the Father's enduring and creative love.

I call you friends

During the 1992 presidential campaign, savvy political pundits bandied about a new term. "F.O.B." ("Friends of Bill") referred to those whose influence and singular loyalty to William Jefferson Clinton distinguished them from the majority of his supporters and well-wishers. In return for their political devotedness, the F.O.B. were privileged to share in special events and interviews with their candidate and were included in the inner circle of revelers at the week-long inaugural extravaganza. But such friendships and the "perks" that accompany them are usually short-lived, dependent as they are upon the unpredictable and often unstable nature of the political climate.

When Jesus addressed his disciples as "friends," he called them to a relationship founded not on shared political interests but on love. Love was to be the constitutive element of the community of believers. Love was to be the new commandment (John 15:12) or new law by which all their words and works would be motivated and through which every thought and deed would be expressed. Moreover, the command of Jesus to his disciples "to love one another" was not simply an arbitrary command intended to promote and ensure social harmony. On the contrary, this mandate was rooted in the very love of Jesus for his own: "as I have loved you." As such, Jesus' call to love one another can be understood as an invitation to the believer to enter into the loving communion shared between Jesus and the Father: "As the Father has loved me, so I have loved you . . . love one another as I have loved you" (John 15:9, 12).

Significantly, Jesus reminded his disciples that their relationship with him (and, therefore, with the Father) was not the result of happenstance. The words, "I *chose* you" (v. 16), underscore the purpose of Jesus' saving mission, viz., to draw all peoples to himself and to the Father. The divine saving intent is also reflected elsewhere in the fourth gospel when Jesus speaks of the Father's *"drawing"* and *"giving"* disciples to Jesus (John 6:37, 44, 65; 17:2, 24).

The extent and fullest expression of Jesus' love was to be shown in the laying down of his life for his friends. Whereas Paul stressed the fact that Jesus "died for us while we were *sinners*" (Romans 8:6, 8, 10), the Johannine author reminds his readers of the dignity and privilege they enjoy by virtue of Jesus' love. The purposeful, loving and saving choice of Jesus transforms those who love and obey him from *slaves* into *friends*. So, also, the revelation of Jesus to his own raises them to a new level of relatedness with him and with the Father ("I call you friends since *I have made known to you* all that I heard from my Father," John 15:15).

"Slave of God" was an honored title for several of Judaism's heroes and patriarchs (Moses, Deuteronomy 34:5; Joshua, Joshua 24:29; David, Psalm 89:20). But Jesus has made possible an even more profound relationship, that of friend. In Hebrew tradition, Abraham was called the friend of God (Isaiah 41:8),

but the Johannine author made it clear that Jesus was even greater than Abraham (John 8:58). Perhaps the evangelist would have his readers recall the narrative earlier in the gospel in which Jesus is proclaimed as the son who would set free those who were *slaves* to sin (John 8:32-36). Jesus' call to friendship also recalls the sapiential text: "Wisdom produces friends of God and prophets. For there is nought God loves, be it not one who dwells with wisdom" (Wisdom 7:27-28). As God's logos (or word and wisdom), Jesus came to empower all people to draw near to the Father in love.

As the result of their loving friendship with him, Jesus' disciples would be sent forth to bear enduring fruit. In other words, their productive and loving lives were to reflect the friendship and love they had come to know in Jesus. Those whose marital relationship is firmly founded in the Lord love one another as friends. Together they reflect the creative, transforming and self-sacrificing love of Jesus for all of humanity.

Unity and glory

The culmination of the lengthy farewell discourse (John 14-17), John 17 represents Jesus' last prayer in which he consecrates himself, his disciples and all future believers to the Father. Largely a Johannine construction, Jesus' consecratory prayer exhibits several parallels to the Lord's Prayer as preserved in the gospels of Matthew and Luke. For example, both prayers: (1) address God as Father, (2) glorify the name of God, (3) express a desire that God's will be done, (4) petition for deliverance from the evil one. But the Johannine prayer of Jesus is also a "carefully wrought exposition of Jesus' legacy to his disciples" (Ernst Käsemann) and is particularly important in illuminating and underscoring the theology of the fourth gospel. The legacy of Jesus, viz., his parting prayer and intention for his disciples, is twofold: he bequeaths *unity* and *glory.*

"That all may be one" (v. 21) calls for a unity among Jesus' future disciples which surpasses a purely social or organizational oneness. Nor is it simply a matter of agreement on moral and/or doctrinal issues. By describing their union with the words, "as you, Father, are in me, and I in you" (v. 21), the Johannine Jesus calls his disciples to share in that ontological union which exists between the Father and the Son.

By virtue of Jesus' legacy of unity, the oneness his disciples are to experience should be *multidimensional. Vertically,* the disciples' union with one another is rooted in and draws life from the loving relationship of Jesus to the Father. *Horizontally,* the disciples' union with and love for one another becomes a force for goodness which reaches out to evangelize the world and to edify and catechize the rest of the believing community. "That the world may believe" and "that the world may know" (vv. 21, 22) are prayerful expressions of the challenge to faith which loving and united disciples can offer to the world. And, *eschatologically,* those who inherit Jesus' legacy of unity live in anticipation of their full and eternal union with the Father.

Glory (the other aspect of Jesus' legacy to his own) is a gift which traces its roots to the first encounters of Israel with Yahweh. As Raymond E. Brown explains, glory is "the visible manifestation of the majesty of God through acts of power." God's glory was first experienced by the newly covenanted nation at Sinai (Exodus 24:16). The glory of the Lord settled on Sinai as a cloud and a consuming fire; thus, the people were aware of Yahweh's active, creative and redeeming presence among them. As the relationship between Yahweh and his people developed, they experienced his glory in the meeting tent (Exodus 40:34) and then in the temple (Ezekiel 43:5). Finally, this glory became flesh and was manifested to humanity in the person and mission of Jesus (John 1:14).

As he approached his "hour" (the reason for which he had come into the world, viz., his saving death and resurrection), the glory of the Father would be fully revealed in Jesus (John 12:23, 13:31). In other words, God's power to save and to draw all peoples to himself in loving forgiveness would become visible in the love of Jesus who lays down his life for his friends (John 15:13). When Jesus bequeathed this glory to his disciples (John 17:22), he thereby mandated his followers to be the "visible manifestation of the majesty of God through acts of power." Just as the glory and presence of God had been revealed in Jesus, so was it to be revealed in the lives of those who believe in him.

Those who live on the brink of the third millennium constitute the future believers for whom Jesus prayed. Those who are the privileged heirs of Jesus' gifts of unity and glory are responsible for the world, so "that the world may believe," "that the world may know," "that the world may love."

PART III

READINGS FOR FUNERALS

First Reading

JOB 19:1, 23-27

I shall see God

*E*ven novice readers of the book of Job are aware that they have happened upon a rare literary and religious treasure; veteran scholars and interpreters have learned that the treasure exists in a veritable minefield of textual corruption and exegetical conflict. Because much of the text has been so poorly preserved or because there are almost 100 *hapax legomena* and countless disputed words, because the authorship and accurate dating of the work remain in dispute, there are as many interpretations of Job as there are interpreters. Nevertheless, the literary quality and timeless, universal themes of Job continue to speak to all of humankind and to guide those who would explore some of life's most elemental questions. Why do the good and the innocent suffer? If God is just, how can these seeming travesties of justice be explained?

Part of Israel's rich tradition of wisdom literature, the plot of Job (viz., the plight of a suffering, innocent person) was probably borrowed from similar folkloric tales which were popular throughout the ancient Near Eastern world. Using this plot to frame his work (Job 1-2, 42:7-17), the Hebrew author couched his basic theological message in a series of poetic dialogues (Job 3:1—42:6). By means of the interchanges between Job, his friends and God, the author enables the reader to foray with him into the controversial doctrine of divine retribution. Finding traditional views inadequate to explain Job's situation, the author then guides his reader to consider an even greater doctrine, viz., the creative power and wisdom of the almighty. As Carol Newsom has explained, "The book of Job is rather like a parable in that it tells a frankly outrageous tale for the purpose of disorienting and reorienting the perspectives of its readers." In the end, Job's persistent and demanding question ("Why?") is sublimated and finessed into an encounter with the "Who?" and the "How?" of the universe.

This short text is one of the most familiar in the book of Job; contextually, it is an excerpt from Job's response to Bildad's second speech. Having already defended God as incapable of acting unjustly (Job 8:1-22), Bildad now warns Job that he will endure the fate of the wicked if he does not examine himself and admit his fault. Vehemently protesting his innocence and describing his suffering and trials as unfair (Job 19:6), Job nevertheless allows his growing insight and faith to pierce through his anger and resentment. Though he can find no logical solution for his situation, he cries out in hope, "I know that my vindicator lives."

Deserted by family and friends, with no one to defend him against the work of the satan, his adversary, Job invokes the ancient tribal kinship law. Calling upon God as his next of kin, Job confidently implores his creator to exercise on his behalf the duties of the *go'el* (vindicator, redeemer), viz., (1) to save him from poverty and assure his posterity, (2) to redeem him from slavery, (3) to protect his life and avenge his death (see Leviticus 25:23-24, 47-55; Ruth 4:1-6).

Unfortunately because the text is so corrupt, it is difficult to ascertain whether Job expected God to act on his behalf *before* or *after* his death. Although it is not well substantiated by the rest of the book, Jerome understood this text (v. 26) as an affirmation of bodily resurrection. This belief, reflected in the Vulgate, was supported by Clement of Rome, Origen and Cyril of Jerusalem. Others disagreed, including Justin, Irenaeus and Tertullian. John Chrysostom wisely and cautiously suggested that this passage speaks not yet of Job's bodily *resurrection* (an idea that appeared only in later Jewish thought, ca. 200 BCE), but of his *healing*. In his exegesis of this difficult and poorly preserved text, R. D. Potter has suggested that v. 26 be read in the conditional tense: "If in my flesh I could see God, him whom I would see would be at my side, in my eyes he would no longer appear as my enemy."

What remains clear in an often unclear passage is the fact of Job's faith and trust in the constant care of God for him. "I know that my vindicator lives" dispels all the false arguments about divine retribution; with these words, Job lifted the pall of suffering and misunderstanding to behold the wisdom and power of the living God.

For all who struggle with the often troubling and unanswerable questions of this imperfect existence, Job's struggle to understand and his growing faith are a source of hope and assurance. Today, as we read Job from the perspective of Jesus' resurrection, we can appreciate the "fuller sense" (sensus plenior) that his words have come to signify for believers. "I know that my vindicator lives . . . and from my flesh I shall see God"— these words have become a reality in the person and mission of Jesus Christ.

Sparks through stubble

No other passage is as certain, no other passage is as unknown as the passage we call death. But Christians find hope in the belief that the passage is not an uncharted one. We who believe in Christ and in his resurrection understand that he has plotted the course through death to life. Although the mid-first century BCE author of Wisdom could not benefit from the words and works of Jesus, nevertheless his notion of death exhibits a radical departure from the traditional view reflected in most of the Jewish scriptures.

For centuries, the author's forebears in the faith ascribed to the belief that all shared the same lot beyond the grave, viz., a vague and nebulous existence apart from God in Sheol. Moreover, there was a general consensus that rewards and/or punishments were meted out in *this* life in accord with divine justice. But in the second century BCE and due in part to the influence of Greek, Egyptian and Persian philosophies, there emerged in Judaism the idea of individual resurrection unto eternal life and of divine retribution for both the just and the wicked after death. The fact that these beliefs were not universal among the Jews is reflected in the New Testament where the Pharisees (who accepted these ideas) and the Sadducees (who rejected them) are portrayed in adversarial positions.

The fact that the author of Wisdom was a Jew of the diaspora (probably Alexandria, Egypt) and well educated in Hellenistic thought is clearly evidenced in this short pericope. His use of Greek literary genre (cynic-stoic diatribe, philosophical inquiry, proof from example) and anthropology is balanced by his firm conviction that true wisdom has its source only in the God of Israel.

In comparing the lot of the wicked with that of the just, the author assures his readers that "the souls of the just are in the hand of God" (v. 1). In Jewish thought, no distinction was made between soul and body. A human being was simply *nephesh*, i.e., a person or self, animated by the life breath of God. Greeks distinguished soul from body and regarded humans as incarnate spirits. Whereas Hellenistic thought attributed immortality to the very nature of the soul, Jewish thought understood immortality as a gift of God to the upright.

Suffering was traditionally regarded as a deserved punishment for some wickedness, but the Wisdom author has reinterpreted the harsh reality of suffering. Rather than punishment, suffering was to be understood as a discipline which teaches and corrects and/or as a test of faith which purifies. Similarly, death was not to be thought of as an affliction or as the destruction of life but as a passage to peace and to God. The peace enjoyed by the souls of the just recalls the post-exilic hopes and visions of Isaiah 57:1-2.

The visitation referred to in v. 7 is a biblical term for divine intervention. In this instance, the reference is to divine judgment which will be exercised after the death of the just as well as of the wicked (Wisdom 14:1). In contrast to the tomblike existence of Sheol, the just will abide in love, blessed with divine grace, mercy and care.

Like "sparks shining through stubble," the lives of those who have been proven faithful to God through suffering and in death light the path and ease the passage for the rest of us who believe.

When the good die young

*I*n the novel *Love Story,* author Erich Segal told the story of Jenny and Oliver, a couple whose life together was cut short by her untimely death. The reader is touched by the sadness and seeming "unfairness" of the lovers' situation. Death is always a difficult passage but it seems somehow less of an affront when the deceased has lived to enjoy many, many years on this earth.

In the ancient world, early death was regarded as a punishment from God for sin; only the wicked were thought to die young, whereas the just were expected to live to old age.

Aware of the views held by his contemporaries, the Wisdom author challenged them to explore with him other possible solutions for the great mystery of death. Part of a longer section (Wisdom 3:1—4:20) in which the author also treats of the suffering of the just and of childlessness, this particular portion of the book of Wisdom refutes the traditional arguments concerning divine retribution. At the same time, the author offers his readers new insight as he invites them to evaluate these issues from the perspective of eternity. Reflected in the author's work is a hope for life with God beyond the grave; this belief emerged in late Jewish thought and literature sometime during the second century BCE. Also reflected in the book of Wisdom is the conviction that the just will enjoy happiness in eternity while the wicked will be punished by God.

Refuting those who regarded death as a curse, the sapiential author promised his readers that the just who die, even at an early age, are at rest. Earlier in the work, he had described their *rest* as being "in the hand of God" (Wisdom 3:1).

Contrary to popular expectation (as per Isaiah 65:20-23), *quality* of life is not to be equated with *quantity* of years. Nor is wisdom (understanding, v. 9) to be necessarily associated with gray hair and advanced years (Proverbs 20:29). Recall the more contemporary saying, "There's no fool like an old fool!"

Verses 10-11 are an historical allusion to Enoch whose death at the comparatively young age of 365 years (as compared to the other patriarchs who were said to live between 700-900 years) was explained in this way: "He walked with God and he was no longer here, for God took him" (see Genesis 5:21-24). Rather than being thought of as a curse and/or a punishment of God, early death could be regarded as a divine rescue from the contamination of a sinful world. As John E. Rybolt has noted, the Wisdom author coined a new term, translated as "whirl of desire" (v. 12), to describe the realm of lust and evil which threatens to corrupt the innocent. Those whose death comes early are snatched away from such dangers. While this notion may do little to assuage the immediate grief of a family and friends (see v. 14), it may eventually be helpful to think that their loved one has been saved from "a fate *worse* than death," viz., life without God.

Finding meaning in an otherwise inexplicable tragedy is never an easy task. But the insight of the Wisdom author guides the believer beyond mere rationality to faith and trust in the eternal source of all wisdom.

Beyond the veil

*F*ew of those who saw the national live telecast in late November 1963 will ever forget the image of Jacqueline B. Kennedy walking slowly behind her dead husband's funeral caisson. A heavy black veil concealed her face but not her grief. Like her veil, a pall of stunned sadness hung over the nation as it mourned with her the death of its young leader and the end of an era which the media had begun to describe as "Camelot."

When the ancient author of this short pericope offered his contemporaries a vision of better times, he spoke of the *destruction* of the veil of death and with it the end of sadness. Part of the so-called Isian apocalypse (Isaiah 24-27), this descriptive text offered hope and encouragement to a people who had been downtrodden by sorrow and suffering. Because of the apocalyptic and/or eschatological themes included in these chapters, most scholars believe they are misplaced in their current context. Rather than an eighth century BCE product, Isaiah 24-27 are probably the work of a later exilic or post-exilic author and belong more properly to the portions of the book attributed to Deutero-Isaiah (chapters 40-55) or Trito-Isaiah (chapters 56-66).

When the Babylonians first invaded the southern kingdom of Judah in 597 BCE, the web (v. 7) of oppression and suffering began to ensnare the nation. By the time Jerusalem fell in 587 BCE, the veil of slavery had completely shrouded all hope for the future. This was the *death* and *reproach* (vv. 7-8) of which the Isian author wrote. For all practical purposes, the nation had died; its leaders were led off to Babylon in chains. In addition to the destruction wrought by Nebuchadnessar's army, Judah's neighbors took advantage of its weakness and plundered its fields and flocks (Obadiah 11). For the next 40 years, the nation that had called itself the chosen people of God lay in the "tomb."

In an attempt to revive his people, the prophetic writer used themes and images borrowed from the antecedent mythologies of neighboring cultures. Informing these motifs with strict Hebrew monotheism, the ancient author offered his contemporaries visions of hope and new life. The great banquet hosted by God on the mountain (Zion?) would celebrate a feast of triumph over death. Like the Canaanite god Baal who swallowed up Mot (the god of death and the underworld), the Lord God of Judah would destroy death and save his people. Significantly, the vision of Isaiah is a universal one, including *all* nations (v. 7).

Gradually, such visions of universal banquets and the end of death and sadness were associated with the era of the messiah-king. When Jesus described in parables the kingdom he had come to establish, he used similar imagery (see, e.g., Matthew 22:2-14, Luke 14:16-24). When the apocalyptic author of Revelation related his visions of the eternal, heavenly Jerusalem, he blessed its inhabitants with similar gifts of life and joy (Revelation 21:3-4).

Each of us has a personal notion of what life will be beyond the veil of death. But, like the ancient author, we share the common belief that the source of all our future happiness and fulfillment is the saving and provident power of God.

Wait and hope

At the end of the turbulent 60s, Swiss psychiatrist Elisabeth Kübler-Ross published her renowned book, *On Death and Dying*. To help her patients and readers navigate the inexorable passage of death and cope with the suffering and anxiety that surround it, Dr. Kübler-Ross suggested that those confronted with death should permit themselves to experience and progress through the stages or attitudes which inevitably factor into the struggle. Two of those stages are anger and grief. Only when these emotions are allowed a healthy expression will peace and acceptance result.

Although the author of Lamentations was not a psychiatrist, he understood the necessity of honesty with oneself and with one's feelings in the face of tragedy. Writing shortly after the destruction of Jerusalem by the Babylonians (ca. 587 BCE), the author of Lamentations gave full vent to the outrage and anguish his contemporaries felt. The destruction of the temple, the interruption of the cult, the exile of the elite of the population, the suppression of national freedom and *sovereignty*—all these losses were tantamount to the experience of death, and all of Judah mourned. As Carroll Stuhlmueller has noted, "This book allows us to remain with grief and tragedy long enough to mourn beauty and goodness as they deserve."

A series of five lamentations written in the *qinah* (dirge) rhythm and arranged in an acrostic (alphabetic) pattern, this biblical work was classified in Jewish tradition among the "Writings" in a section called *Megilloth* (scrolls) and was read on special feasts. In later Judaism, the book of Lamentations was prayed on the Ninth of Ab (July-August) to commemorate the destruction of the first temple in 587 BCE, the second temple in 70 CE and the last stronghold of Bar Cochba in 135 CE.

In the first two laments, the author reprised the figure of Israel as the bride of Yahweh (as per the prophets). But in Lamentations, the bride has become a widow, bereft of every earthly blessing. Her description of the horror and devastation included a reference to conditions so extreme that some were forced to resort to cannibalism (Lamentations 2:20, 4:10).

Six centuries later, another conqueror wreaked similar havoc on Israel. There is poignant significance in the fact that, when the emperor Vespasian wished to memorialize his son Titus' conquest of Jerusalem (70 CE), he struck a coin depicting *Nike* (Victory) standing over the body of a female figure representing *Judea Capta* ("Captured Judah"). The bride who had become a widow was now a slave.

But Lamentations is not an unmitigated wail of sorrow and despair. Indeed, like other laments that appear throughout the Hebrew scriptures, the grief and anger expressed in Lamentations has been thoroughly infused with faith in God's presence and trust in his power to save. As Michael Guinan has explained, the situation of devastation in Jerusalem left the Israelites with three options. They could: (1) return to their perennial fascination with the Canaanite gods, or (2) worship the gods of Babylon who appeared to be stronger than Yahweh (some believed this accounted for the fact that Babylon had prevailed over Israel), or (3) remain faithful to Yahweh and endeavor to resolve their problems in his presence. Lamentations represents Israel's choice of the third option as well as its struggle to make it work.

In the third lamentation, outrage and sorrow yield to trust and acceptance. As reflected in this pericope, the one who has been mourning the loss of every earthly possession has also remembered that the Lord's favors and mercies (*hesed* and *rahamin*, v. 22), constant and reliable in the past (v. 21), are also an inexhaustible source of hope for the future. The triple declaration of "good" things (vv. 25-27) enunciates the sufferer's acceptance of his situation and his renewed desire for commitment to the Lord. "To bear the yoke" (v. 27) is a graphic expression for doing the will of God (see Jeremiah 2:20). Content to wait (v. 25) and hope in silence for salvation (v. 26), the people have turned from bitter complaint to peaceful compliance.

When ancient Christians mourned the sufferings and death of Jesus during Holy Week, they sang sections of Lamentations during the tenebrae (darkness) services. Today, Lamentations can continue to express the grief, outrage, hope and trust of suffering, faith-filled believers.

Life is forever

---

*T*hroughout its history, humankind has entertained a variety of notions with regard to the afterlife. A particularly odd slant on the subject appeared in a letter to a deceased person from the South Carolina Department of Social Services: "Your food stamps will be stopped effective March 1992, because we received notice that you passed away. May God bless you. You may reapply if there is a change in your circumstances." Dark humor notwithstanding, this notice nevertheless reflects a somewhat vague understanding that death is *not* the final chapter in human life; indeed, the belief in the continuance of some sort of existence after death has been integral to the Judeo-Christian tradition since the second century BCE.

Most of the Old Testament, however, reveals little hope of individual survival after death. Sheol, or the underworld, is mentioned as the place where the dead (both good and evil) lie in an inert, nebulous state. Although certain texts (Isaiah 26:19, Hosea 6:2, Ezekiel 37) refer metaphorically to the *restoration* to life of Israel as a corporate entity, belief in individual resurrection appeared only in later Hebrew writings, and most of these references were in books the Jews considered non-canonical (e.g., Wisdom, Maccabees, Enoch). Nevertheless, this text from Daniel which appeared ca. 165 BCE is the earliest undisputed reference to individual resurrection; as such, it represents one of the book of Daniel's major contributions to Jewish and Christian theologies.

Apocalyptic literature written during the persecution of the Jews by Antiochus IV Epiphanes, Daniel is a combination of short stories (Daniel 1-6) and visions (Daniel 7-12) intended to edify and encourage the persecuted with promises of victory and vindication. With the stories of other Jewish heroes who withstood their oppressors, the author wished to bolster the courage of his contemporaries to remain faithful to their own religious heritage despite the onslaught of Hellenization.

Combined with the visions of a better day, these stories communicate the central theme of Daniel, viz., that Yahweh, the God of Israel, is the Lord of human history; his reign is not relegated to the faroff future but is an effective aspect of human endeavor in every age. For those who felt abandoned by God and left to fend for themselves in an increasingly hostile world, Daniel offered hope and solace.

In this particular text, the faithful are assured that they shall survive the "time unsurpassed in distress" (v. 1). The historian Arnold J. Toynbee used this phrase from Daniel to describe those recurring periods of suffering in the lives of people of every society in every age. As history attests, each generation thinks of their own time as this "time of distress." The words of Daniel which comforted the persecuted Jews of the second century BCE reach out across the centuries to console all who suffer: Your names have been inscribed by God in the book (i.e., of life, as in Exodus 32:32-33, Psalm 69:29).

A poetic way of expressing God's gift of life to humanity, this remarkable text further assures the faithful of resurrection unto *everlasting life* (v. 2). The first reference to eternal life in the scriptures, the "cogency of this belief in Daniel derives from an underlying trust in divine retribution" (John J. Collins). The righteous who suffer for their faith and who lose their lives in this world shall live forever in the next. Moreover, their cause will be defended by God's own emissaries. Michael the great prince (v. 1), also known in the Qumran literature (1 QS 3:24, 1 QS 3:20) as the Angel of Truth or the Prince of Light, was Israel's special patron and guardian angel.

Notice that both the wicked and the just will be raised. The wicked will reap the everlasting harvest of disgrace which their evil ways have sown, but the just will shine like stars forever. A common theme in Jewish apocalyptic, the goodness of those whose wisdom derives from the God of Israel (as opposed to those who pursue wisdom in pagan sources, e.g., Hellenism) will be "seven times as brilliant as the sun" (2 Enoch 66:7). The just or the wise (*maskilim*) were understood as those whose faith-filled words and works have enlightened and inspired others to live good lives ("who lead the many to justice," v. 3).

Each of us has loved and lost someone whose goodness has brought joy and hope into our lives. For those who believe, their goodness is not dead nor are they lost. They live and shine forever with the Lord.

They rest in godliness

Lex orandi, lex credendi. This Latin axiom (literally translated: "The rule of prayer is the rule of belief") has been an accepted theological norm since the fifth century CE. Although the phrase can be traced to the *Indiculus,* composed by Prosper of Aquitaine (d. 460 CE), the gist of the term can be found in the writings of Augustine (d. 430 CE) and, before him, in those of Tertullian (d. 220 CE) and Cyprian (d. 258 CE). This long-standing, sound principle illustrates the understanding that the faith of the believing community is rooted in and expressed by the prayer of the community. That principle is at the heart of this short pericope from the second book of the Maccabees.

Writing during the last quarter of the second century BCE, the author of 2 Maccabees wished to edify his contemporaries and to encourage them in their struggle to remain faithful to their religious heritage. Underlying the stories of Jewish heroes and their battles with the pagan oppressors was a polemic against the author's own detractors and opponents. Sympathetic to the cause and beliefs of the orthodox Hasidim (1 Maccabees 2:42) who were the forerunners of the Pharisees and Essenes, the author supported and instructed his readers in the doctrines of the resurrection of the dead and of divine retribution for both the just and the wicked (2 Maccabees 7:9, 11, 14, 23; 14:46). He also struggled against the Hellenizing influences within the priesthood which was largely composed of Sadducees who rejected any belief in the afterlife. Perhaps this conflict contributed to the author's clear and unequivocal enunciation of faith in the individual resurrection of the body.

According to the narrative (2 Maccabees 12:38-42), Judas Maccabeus and his soldiers were preparing to bury their fellow soldiers who had been killed in one of the many battles with the Syrians. Finding pagan amulets on the bodies of the slain, Judas presumed that the men had died because they had breached the law (the law forbade Jews to wear such amulets or to take them as booty in battle).

Praising God for his justice, Judas then advised his soldiers to avoid such sin in their own lives. Thoroughly Deuteronomic in his theology, the author underscored, through his protagonist Judas, his conviction that sin breached the law and the covenant with God and led to punishment. Repentance, on the other hand, led to restoration of the covenant relationship and to salvation.

So certain was his belief in the resurrection of the dead that Judas organized an expiatory sacrifice to atone for the sins of those who had fallen in battle. Prayers for the deceased were believed to have efficacy because they were indeed alive in the Lord.

The faith in individual resurrection expressed in this pericope exhibits a marked development over most of the Hebrew scriptures. Up until the second century BCE, the concept of Sheol as a place of finality or as a holding place (1 Enoch 22:12-13) pervaded Hebrew thought. But here, in the Maccabean literature and in its account of a nation's courageous fight for religious and political freedom, we find profound insights into life, suffering, death and survival. These insights were born of faith in a saving, provident and just God; these insights gave birth to a prayer that was rich in confidence and hope for the future.

Lex orandi, lex credendi . . . *for over 20 centuries, the believing community has given powerful voice to its faith in immortality. This prayer reaches beyond the grave and shares in the victory and joy of the faithful who have gone before us.*

NB. While the Maccabean insights into immortality were accepted by the Pharisaic Jews and later by Christians, they were rejected by the Sadducees, and the Maccabean literature did not gain acceptance in the Jewish canon. In later centuries, Christian theologians referred to this pericope as a source-text for their development of the doctrine of purgatory. The reformers (ca. 1530 CE), championed by Luther, Melancthon, Calvin and Zwingli, rejected the canonicity of Maccabees

and, with it, the doctrine of purgatory and the appropriate-
ness of prayers for the dead.

Second Reading

ACTS 10:34-43

No partiality

One of the biggest blights on the history of the United States is the fact that this nation, founded on the principles of justice and freedom for all, allowed discrimination (or worse) against some of its citizens because of the color of their skin. In total abnegation of the vision of the founding fathers, recognized authorities not only tolerated prejudice but upheld and enforced it.

Segregation prevailed in restaurants and on public transportation. Water fountains were restricted according to race; hotels refused to provide shelter for the black entertainers who performed there. Blacks and whites attended different schools and churches (some churches which permitted blacks relegated them to back pews or the choir loft). I can even recall a time when, in some areas of the country, black Catholics were permitted to approach the altar to receive the eucharist only after all the whites had received. And, as if to prove that prejudice is a monster that refuses to die, black people were buried in separate cemeteries or separate areas of the same cemetery in which whites were buried.

But Americans are not the only people who have permitted such practices to pervert the integrity of their faith; similar issues provided the setting for this pericope from the Acts of the Apostles.

Featuring Peter on the occasion of his visit to Cornelius' home, this text underscores the *universal* scope of God's plan of salvation. Revealed in the words and works of Jesus, this plan was to be furthered by the subsequent universal mission of the church. The good news ("word," v. 36) that had been first extended to Israel (Isaiah 52:7) and which was the essence of Jesus' earthly work was also to be extended to every nation because "God shows no partiality" (v. 34). Although largely a Lucan composition (as were other similar speeches in Acts), this sermon represents a change in policy and a growth in understanding on the part of the early Jewish Christians, represented by Peter.

Cornelius was a Roman soldier, a centurion stationed in Caesarea. He was a God-fearer, i.e., one who ascribed to Israel's strict monotheistic beliefs, but he was nevertheless a gentile and did not adhere to Jewish food laws or rituals of purification. Ordinarily, Jews did not accept or offer hospitality to gentiles because the association would have rendered them unclean. But Peter had been divinely prepared for his meeting with Cornelius: By means of a pedagogical vision, Peter learned that he "should not call any person profane or unclean" (Acts 10:11-16, 28).

Peter's acceptance of Cornelius and his subsequent approbation of the gentile mission represented a landmark decision within the early Christian community. While not readily accepted by certain elements within the church (see Acts 11:1-18), this decision nevertheless reflected the belief that those who were committed to Christ were thereby called to supersede every barrier, limitation and obstacle which might otherwise impede or threaten their union.

Christ's saving death did not discriminate. His forgiveness and healing were not limited or selective but were extended to all. The church which professes him as risen Lord and shares in the fullness of his life can do no less.

While still sinners

Whenever I read the letter of Paul to the Romans and study his insights into the good news of our justification through faith in Jesus Christ, I am reminded (oddly enough) of the well-known children's story, *The Little Engine Who Could.* "I think I can, I think I can," puffed the little engine as it persevered up a steep grade. Finally, only after a valiant effort, the engine reached the top of the incline and coasted down the other side. The moral of the little tale was that will power, self-confidence and hard work assured success. In a sense, this was a fairly accurate evaluation of the Hebrew notion of justification prior to the appearance of Jesus Christ.

As E. P. Sanders has explained in the recently published, *The Romans Debate* (chapter 20), Judaism's religious self-understanding was *initially* based "on the premise of grace—that God had freely chosen and made his covenant with Israel—to be their God and they his people." Nevertheless, by Paul's day, that focus had become dissipated by the multiplicity of laws. Justification and/or righteousness became equated with a fastidious interpretation and application of the law in its seemingly innumerable precepts. This focus on personal effort and achievement was completely reversed by the revelation of the good news of salvation in Jesus Christ (Romans 1:16). Because of his conversion to Christ, Paul learned that his "I think I can" mentality had to be transformed into an "I trust in you" posture of receptivity toward God. This adjusted attitude reflects the understanding that salvation is not a reward for a job well done but an undeserved *gift* from a gracious, forgiving Father. In this pericope from Romans, Paul explores the wondrousness of that gift.

No longer is the law the criterion for justification; rather, the "love of God" (v. 5) is the reason for and motivation behind the saving mission of Jesus. Notice that Paul refers to God's love as having been "poured out," thereby avoiding any notion of a quid pro quo exchange of love for obedience to the law. Moreover, the lavish and extravagant gifts were offered to the "powerless" (v. 6), viz., to "sinners" (v. 8). Using the example of one human being offering his/her life for another, Paul admitted that, in some rare instances, it is *conceivable* that one might perform such a heroic act for a "good" or "just" person (v. 7). But God has proven his exceeding love for us by the almost incredible fact that Christ died for us precisely when we were not "good" or "just." As John Paul Heil has explained, "It is this extreme and abundant love of God, now effusively poured into our hearts, that continually sustains our Christian hope . . . so that it never disappoints us in any way."

Earlier in this letter, Paul had associated justification (or being right with God) with Christ's resurrection (Romans 4:25). Here (v. 9), he ascribes it to Jesus' blood, i.e., to his death. Paul's Jewish readers understood that the shedding of sacrificial blood was necessary for expiation, purification, atonement and the sealing of the sacred bond of the covenant (Hebrews 9:22). To achieve those ends, animal sacrifices were offered. But in Jesus' saving sacrifice, the blood was not that of an animal; it was his very own life poured out to reconcile sinners with the Father. Through his blood, sins are atoned, sinners are purified and the covenantal relationship is forever renewed.

Notice that Paul speaks of the savings gifts of God as a present experience ("we have been justified," v. 9) as well as an eschatological process ("we shall be saved by him," v. 9). Elsewhere, Paul referred to the believer's engagement in the process of salvation as "putting on the Lord Jesus Christ" (Romans 13:14).

Paul's exuberance is obvious as he calls believers to "boast." This is the third call to boasting issued by the great apostle. First, he advocated boasting in hope for the glory of God (Romans 5:2); then, boasting in our afflictions (5:3); here, he calls for boasting of God himself (5:11).

To boast of God as our hope and salvation is to acknowledge him as the source and center of our existence, the one who has effected our justification by reconciling us to himself in Christ. To boast of God is to relinquish the self-reliant, self-centered "I think I can," and to humbly, gratefully confess, "I trust in you, O Lord."

Much more in Christ

*D*uring the 15th and 16th centuries, morality plays were a popular and instructive mode of religious expression. The characters in the plays were personifications of certain *attributes,* such as *Hope, Faith, Envy,* etc. One of the classic examples of the morality play was the anonymous work called *Everyman* whose title character found himself deserted by all except *Good Deeds* while *Death* threatened his demise. In this pericope from his letter to the Romans, Paul has similarly dramatized the story of our salvation.

In setting the scene and assigning the roles of the protagonists, Paul's main purpose was to contrast the influence of Adam upon humankind with that of Jesus Christ. In addition to these two key figures, the story also includes *Anthropos (Humanity), Hamartia (Sin), Thanatos (Death), Charis (Grace)* and *Nomos (Law).* As the drama unfolds, the reader-observer is challenged to discover and understand in himself/herself the consequences of sin and the effects of redemption.

Two basic concepts which underlie Paul's graphic presentation must be appreciated for full understanding of his theology. The first is the Hebrew notion of corporate personality or solidarity whereby Adam is portrayed not simply as one private individual but as the Everyman of humankind. Through him, sin and its consequences were unleashed to wreak havoc in the world. Paul's statement, "just as a single offense brought condemnation to all men" (v. 18), must be understood in this light. Recall also Paul's earlier explanation that human beings ratified Adam's sin in their *own* lives through *personal* sin (Romans 5:12).

Although the *Law* was introduced as a divine guide to lead *Humanity* to life (Leviticus 18:5), it nevertheless became a catalyst for *Sin* in that it gave a clearer knowledge of personal obligation without providing the means to fulfill those duties. For the sinner, the law functioned as informer, accuser and instructor in evil.

A secondary underlying concept is the notion that death is a direct consequence of sin. Paul understood that *Death* had begun to reign in the world as a consequence of Adam's offense (v. 17). But Adam also served as a type of the ultimate human being, viz., Jesus Christ, whose action ended the reigns of *Sin* and *Death* and inaugurated the reign of *Grace*. Notice, whereas Adam's action led to death, the saving activity of Jesus results in eternal life (v. 21).

Key to the entire drama of human history is the Greek phrase *pollo mallon* (v. 17) which means "much more." Regardless of how devastating the influence of *Sin* is, the saving power of Jesus is *much more;* Christ's saving deeds are far superior to the sinful effect of Adam.

Paul's drama of salvation encourages optimism and trust for those whose daily conflict with Sin *continues. For those believers whose earthly struggle has come to an end,* Death *is no longer an enemy to be feared. Because of* Christ *and through his* Grace, Death *has simply become a passage to* Life.

Death has no power

William Shakespeare's *Hamlet* describes death as "the undiscover'd country from whose bourn no traveller returns" (III, i). Over two millennia before Shakespeare, the author of Genesis expressed a similar air of finality concerning the end of human life: "For you are dust and to dust you shall return" (Genesis 3:19). This same sense of dread and dissolution with regard to death is woven throughout the Hebrew scriptures and has been given eloquent expression in the liturgical and sapiential literature of ancient Israel (Psalm 90:3, 103:14; Ecclesiastes 3:20, 12:7; Wisdom 15:8; Sirach 10:9, 17:2; Job 10:9, 34:15). Death was considered to be the work of Adam whose disobedience to God unleashed sin and its lethal consequences upon humanity. Using these ideas and beliefs as his starting point, Paul proceeded to lift the pall which hung upon the world so as to preach the good news of Jesus Christ. By his victory over sin, Jesus robbed death of its power; because of his victory, all who believe can look upon death, not as the end of life but as a *passage* to life everlasting.

Part of a longer section of his letter to Rome, in which Paul details the *consequences* of Christ's death, this particular pericope focuses on baptism as the means by which believers *participate* in Jesus' saving activity. Reminding the Roman Christians of the catechesis which had prepared them for receiving the sacrament ("Are you not aware," v. 3), Paul explained that believers are baptized *"eis Christon,"* i.e., *into* Christ. In other words, Christians are not simply identified with the death of Jesus; but believers are, through baptism, introduced into the very process of Jesus' dying.

As Eugene Maly has observed, the preposition "into" is followed by the noun "Christ" in the accusative; this "indicates a movement into the person so that one can speak of incorporation." In Romans 5, Paul described death as a consequence of sin, but the death of Jesus was different. Since he had no sin, his death was the consequence of his *obedience*; by so embracing the Father's will, Jesus gave new meaning to death. No longer regarded as a *consequence* of sin, Jesus' obedient death is to be understood as a *rejection* of sin. Those who are buried with him are called to a similar obedience and a similar rejection of sin. The "old self" (v. 6), viz., the human person affected by and prone to sin through Adam, must die. Paul employed special terminology for explaining the believer's participation in Christ's death. "Crucified with" Christ, i.e., to sin and to its power, the believer is thereby "freed from sin" (vv. 6-7). A difficult phrase, *dedikaiotai* ("freed from sin") is derived from a Jewish legal maxim which declared a dead person acquitted of all debts and further litigation. Having been thus declared dead to sin and free of its debts (death, alienation from God, etc.), the believer is also empowered to share in Christ's resurrection.

Notice that the efficient cause or initiative for the resurrection of Jesus is attributed to the Father and to his glory (v. 4). Just as in the Hebrew scriptures, the glory of God was credited for all the saving wonders enjoyed by Israel (Exodus 15:7, 11; 16:7, 10), so, too, in the Christian dispensation, the *doxa* (Greek) or *kabod* (Hebrew) of God is the agent of salvation. Manifested in Jesus' death and rising, the glory of God empowers the believer who dies with Christ to "live a new life, here and now" (v. 4), and to enjoy a "like resurrection" (v. 5) throughout eternity.

For those who believe, death has no power; death can wield no fear. In this, the dying find strength and hope. In this belief, those who mourn their dead find comfort.

Abba!

---

*T*he community to which Paul addressed his longest letter was no stranger to class distinctions. Those with the highest status in Roman society were the senators. Six hundred in number, the members of the senate controlled the empire's finances, foreign policy and military operations. Among the equestrian class were included wealthy individuals who administered the collection of revenues, conducted business and served as officers in the army and as governors over the provinces. Free citizens who were not of the senatorial or equestrian classes formed a "third estate." These were considerably poorer than the upper classes and made their living as soldiers, farmers or artisans. Another class in Roman society was composed of slaves; during the reign of Trajan, slaves comprised one third of Rome's population.

Aware of the Roman experience, Paul called believers in that city to recognize the fact that, because of Christ, they had been gifted with a new and unique status, viz., they were privileged to be *children of God.*

In chapter five of his letter to Rome, Paul had begun to recount the effects of justification enjoyed by believers. In chapter eight, while focusing on the indwelling of the Spirit, Paul explored the new relationship afforded to believers in Christ and the rights and responsibilities concomitant with that relationship. Using the technical legal term for adoption (*huiothesia*), Paul assured believers in Rome that their new status was an *official* one which guaranteed their freedom from slavery (to fear, to the law, to sin, to death) and assured them a share in the very relationship which Jesus shared with the Father. To that end, Christians may call upon God in the same intimate manner Jesus did. "Abba" was the Aramaic term of intimacy for one's father. Unique to Jesus (Mark 14:36), this privilege is now shared by those who have been adopted as God's own children. The verb *krazein* ("cry," v. 15) appears frequently in the prayers of Israel and refers to the various and sundry circumstances of life in which the believer is wont to call upon God (Psalm 3:5, 17:6, 88:2, 19, etc.). The verb can also mean "to cry aloud in proclamation." In either meaning, crying "Abba" is to be understood as a special form of communication reserved for God's own children.

With the new status of adoption, believers become heirs; as heirs, they will be privileged to share in the estate of the Father which is *glory*. However, just as the path to glory for Jesus led him through a course of suffering, so shall those who are children and heirs with Christ trace the same path.

Ascribing to the biblical concept of solidarity, Paul explained that, just as the created universe was affected by human sin (Genesis 3:17), so also does the material world share humanity's hope for renewal, healing and reconciliation (Isaiah 11:6-9, 66:22; Amos 9:13). As part of a global ecosystem, humanity can both corrupt and preserve its environment. Today's scientists point to the physical and observable effects of humanity's use or misuse of the earth. But Paul would have us be aware that ethical, spiritual and moral attitudes of humankind also exert powerful influences upon the universe. As such, the universe becomes a reflection of the human soul.

Underscoring the proleptic aspect of redemption, viz., that it is a process which is begun in us and in which we participate until its culmination, Paul acknowledged the necessity of yearning and even groaning for fulfillment. Believers, led by the Spirit, experience the status of adopted children of God here and now (v. 14) but, in the eschatological endtime, they shall know the fullness of that relationship with Jesus and the Father in glory (v. 23).

*P*aul's comparison of present suffering to future glory encourages all who struggle to live as worthy heirs of God; encouraged, too, are those who mourn the passing of a loved one. No matter how great their pain and suffering had been, it pales into insignificance before the joy and glory they shall know with the Father. Dag Hammarskjold, the late secretary general of the United Nations, obviously shared Paul's faith and hope. In his spiritual journal, *Markings*, he reflected upon his life with its share of suffering and trial. As he looked ahead with *hope to a better future, he prayed, "For all that has been, thanks; for all that will be, yes!"*

God is for us!

When *Hebrew* parents wish to pass on to their children their understanding of God, they begin with the exodus event. The fact that their ancestors passed from slavery to freedom through the power of Yahweh is the focal point of their experience and knowledge of God. Through that pivotal event, ancient Israelites had come to identify themselves as a people, related by covenant to a caring, protective, sustaining and liberating God. Every subsequent moment of their national and spiritual history was interpreted in reference to the exodus and to the mighty God who had made their passage a reality. Whenever Israel was tempted to doubt or question the power and presence of their God, they evoked the memory of the exodus and their faith was renewed. Every year, Jewish people all over the world celebrate their ancient passage to freedom so as to hand on the meaning of the event to future generations.

When *Christian* parents share with their children their sacred traditions, they look to another passover, viz., that achieved by Jesus Christ through his suffering, death and resurrection. Just as the ancient exodus achieved liberation, identity and blessings for Israel, so, too, did Christ's victory over death empower believers to live free of sin and thereby enjoy a new life in the Spirit. If ever Christians are plagued with doubt or discouragement, they have only to remember the incredible and immeasurable gift God has given them in his Son. It was this fact which Paul recalled for the Romans and which he celebrates in this wonderful hymn of salvation. Using terms intended to invoke the willingness of Abraham to sacrifice Isaac, i.e., "did not spare his own son" (as per Genesis 22:2, 12), Paul explained that, if God had already given the greatest gift possible, then believers had a sure guarantee that God will oversee and anticipate all their other needs as well.

Beginning in Romans 5, Paul had painstakingly elaborated all the blessings enjoyed by believers as a result of their justification by Christ. With this pericope, he draws the whole lesson together in a moving and dramatic display of verbal fireworks. Through a series of rhetorical questions (vv. 33-35), Paul makes it clear that there is nothing that can come between believers and the love which God has for them in Christ. Assuming the attitude and tone of a defense attorney in a court of law, Paul virtually dares anyone to present evidence to refute him.

Listing a series of possible obstacles (e.g., trial, distress, persecutions, etc.), all of which Paul had personally endured, he declares himself and all believers to be "more than conquerors because of him who has loved us" (v. 37). These words reminded Paul's Roman readers, who were already being victimized by the wrath of the empire, that no earthly power could rob them of the gifts of God or demean their status as God's own beloved children.

In this hymn's last two verses, Paul listed even further possible obstacles or limits to God's love. Angels, principalities and powers represent various ranks of spiritual beings, some of whom were considered hostile to humanity. These, declared Paul, have no power. Nor does anything present or to come. Height and depth are astrological terms which designate the supposed influence of stars, etc., depending upon their remoteness or proximity to earth. Even these mysterious influences, says Paul, cannot separate us from the love of God.

Those who believe live in Christ, having died with him to sin and death. Death is no longer the last stop on life's journey but a passage to even fuller life and love.

In life and in death, we are the Lord's

Born in Florence, Italy, in 1265, Dante Alighieri received a classical education and became active in politics while still a young man. Because he opposed Pope Boniface VIII, his property was confiscated. He was exiled and condemned to death in absentia. While in exile, he wrote his *Divine Comedy*. Considered his greatest work, it leads its reader on an imaginary tour through hell (*Inferno*), purgatory (*Purgatorio*) and heaven (*Paradiso*).

On the way through hell, Dante detailed a roster of the damned, many of whom were politicians, artists and religious leaders of his day. While this journey represented the author's effort to come to grips with his personal calamities and weaknesses (as well as those of his nation), nevertheless, Dante seemed to allow himself, albeit through the realm of literary imaginings, a prerogative which belongs solely to God, viz., that of passing judgment on other persons. Although this same injustice had been perpetrated against Dante, nevertheless, as Paul explains in his letter to the Romans, "we are responsible to the Lord" and it is to him alone that "everyone of us will have to give an account" (14:8, 12).

Occasioned by disputes over differing religious ideals and practices (e.g., conservatives versus liberals), this pericope is excerpted from a longer exhortation in which Paul urged the Roman Christians to refrain from judging one another (Romans 14:4). Concern for harmonious and healthy interpersonal relations within the community should override any desire of the members to set themselves up as arbiters of one another's consciences. Those who belong to the Lord are to forego all such detrimental activities, realizing that their shared faith and common commitment to Christ call forth a nobler way of life.

Living and dying as one's own master (v. 7) meant to conduct oneself independently and in total self-reliance. "He/she is his/her own person" was considered as much a compliment in ancient Rome's secular society as it is in today's. But, as Paul proclaims, "we are the Lord's" and this precludes all self-centered indulgence and self-sufficiency.

Through his saving death and glorious resurrection, Jesus Christ has become Lord of the universe and of all the living and the dead. Those who have become justified by faith in Christ live and die no longer solely unto themselves but in him.

This special relationship with Christ draws all those who believe into a special relationship with one another as well. As the poet John Donne declared, "No man is an island." Islands are solitary and separate; but those who belong to Christ in faith are also the children of Abraham whose descendants were promised to be as numerous as the grains of sand on the seashore (Genesis 22:17). Just as the sands shift with the wind and the tides, shaping and adapting themselves to the shoreline, so should the believer be conformed to Christ.

Adapting themselves to the principles of the good news, Christians are also called to yield to one another for the sake of Christ. The respect and consideration of believers for one another does not diminish their self-identity. On the contrary, those who live altruistically (as did Jesus, the "man for others" par excellence) fully realize their identity in solidarity with one another in Christ.

Within this matrix of respect and mutual consideration, even those with the most diverse and pluralistic ideals and life-styles can survive and flourish. Within this matrix of communal support, judgment of both the living and the dead is relegated to God alone.

Those who anticipate the prerogative of God to hold accountable and to judge have not yet perceived the fundamental message of the cross: "God proves his love for us in that, while we were still sinners, Christ died for us" (Romans 5:8).

All will live again

Within the past few years, a game called *Jenga* has enjoyed popularity among children and adults. The object of the game is to remove one piece of wood from among the many pieces which fit together to form a rectangular tower, without toppling the tower. If a player mistakenly removes a supporting piece and the tower falls, the player loses the game. In Paul's letter to the church at Corinth, he described the resurrection in similar terms. A fundamental doctrine, the resurrection is a linchpin for the entire construct of belief in Jesus. Without it, Christian faith collapses.

Like other Christians of Greek background, the Corinthians had particular difficulty with the notion of resurrection because of the dualism that characterized their basic philosophical and anthropological ideas. Matter (and, therefore, the body) was regarded as evil; the soul or spirit was valued as good. According to the Greek sages, "The body is a tomb" and "I am a poor soul shackled to a corpse." Immortality consisted in ridding oneself of the body; therefore, resurrection of the body was tantamount to absurdity.

There were also some Christians in Corinth who regarded themselves as an elite and spiritual people (1 Corinthians 2:6—3:4) who *already* enjoyed eternal life. These also rejected the resurrection as having no significance for them. In 1 Corinthians 15, the most complete exploration of the resurrection in the Christian scriptures, Paul presented his argument in three stages. First, he outlined the traditions of eschatology and the confession of the resurrection inherited by believers (1 Corinthians 15:12-19). Then he appealed to scripture (vv. 20-28). Finally, he concluded with a series of ad hominem arguments (vv. 29-34), all of which he set in the framework of a diatribe.

This pericope represents Paul's effort to find a scriptural foundation for his argument (1 Corinthians 15:25, 27 allude to Psalm 110:1 and Psalm 8:7). With the term *dei* ("must," v. 25), Paul assured his readers that all that has happened for Jesus and all that is yet to be fulfilled for believers are *necessary* and integral to God's saving plan for humanity.

Referring to the Jewish ritual of offering the initial products of field and flock to God, Paul explained that the risen Jesus is the "firstfruits of those who have fallen asleep" (v. 20). The offering of the firstfruits signified the consecration of the entire harvest to God. Similarly, Jesus has made sacred in his death and resurrection the entire harvest of humanity. As the "firstfruits," his rising to glory is a pledge and sure promise of the life and glory every believer will share.

Citing that solidarity between Adam and the rest of humanity which brought sin and death into the world, Paul underscored the fact that our solidarity in Christ effects an even greater reality, viz., *life* and a place in the eternal kingdom.

Rather than ascribe to a dualistic or elitist understanding of themselves, Paul urged the Corinthians to develop an anthropology which was essentially christological: Jesus Christ has died and is now raised to life; he is the *firstfruits* and the *pledge* of what *we* shall be, alive forever to God in Christ Jesus.

Paul understood the reality of Jesus' resurrection as an event in the process of being fully realized throughout all creation. The victory over death of the risen Lord is the substance of our faith and the source of meaning for life here and now. While we await his second coming, we rejoice in the hope that his gift of life is more powerful than sin and stronger than death.

1 CORINTHIANS 15:51-57

We will be changed

Whenever Paul preached about the risen Jesus and the consequences of his resurrection for believers, he received a variety
of responses. So enthusiastic were some of the Thessalonians
that they quit their jobs. They were determined to wait for the
Lord's return and to experience their share in his risen glory.
Others in that same city stirred up an angry mob and accused
Paul of sedition (2 Thessalonians 3:6-15, Acts 17). Some of
those to whom Paul preached were swayed by false teachers who
attacked him and his gospel; others, like Lydia, became staunch
believers and put all their earthly goods at the service of the
growing Christian community (Galatians 1:6-9, Acts 16:14-15).

When Paul spoke to the Athenians in the Areopagus,
some of the curious who enjoyed the titillation of novel and
different ideas heard him out and then branded him a "mag-
pie." Others misunderstood his preaching about Jesus and the
resurrection and thought he referred to Jesus and a goddess
named Anastasis (Greek for "resurrection"). Still others sneered
at the very notion of the resurrection of the dead and told Paul
to come back and try again another day (Acts 17:22-32). Nevertheless, Paul was not daunted and through him many came to
believe. The basis of their faith, like Paul's, was the reality of
Jesus who died on the cross and rose to life everlasting.

In this short pericope which concludes his lengthy exposition on the resurrection (1 Corinthians 15), Paul responds to
the question, "How are the dead raised? With what kind of
body will they come back?" (1 Corinthians 15:35). Unlike the
Greeks with their dualistic philosophy and anthropology, Paul
did not believe that salvation was a *release* of the soul from
the body but a *redemption* of the whole human person, body
and spirit. He also based his understanding of the resurrection of the believer on what he had come to know of the risen
Lord: "The one who raised Christ from the dead will give life
to your mortal bodies also" (Romans 8:11).

But what kind of body shall it be? It is clear that Paul understood resurrection to be a *transformation* of the human person and not merely a *resuscitation*: "We shall be changed" (v. 52). The new life we shall experience is not to be like that of Lazarus who was called forth from the grave to resume his life as it had been. Rather, those who rise in Christ will be clothed with incorruptibility and immortality.

Just as our salvation is a totally unmerited gift, so shall our transformation into eternal life be effected by the power of God. Like his contemporaries, Paul hoped that the return of Christ would occur while many of those to whom he ministered were still alive (v. 51). Infusing his expectation with the symbols of Jewish apocalypticism, he awaited the sound of the last trumpet (Joel 2:1, Zephaniah 1:16, 4 Ezra 6:23). When it sounded, all would be transformed, not as the result of a labored evolutionary process but "in the twinkling of an eye."

Because speaking of life after death and of a continued existence outside the parameters of time and space defies empirical reason and challenges even the most erudite vocabulary, Paul acknowledged that he was communicating a *mystery* (v. 51). For Paul, a mystery was a "secret, hidden in God for long ages and now revealed, a new revelation about God's salvation" (Joseph Fitzmyer). Throughout his letters, Paul described God's mystery as Jesus Christ, crucified and risen for the salvation of humanity.

Here, in this pericope from his letter to Corinth, he reveals the fact that God's mystery will include a share in Christ's victory for all who believe. Because of Jesus, Hosea's prophecy of doom for Israel (Hosea 13:14) has been transformed into a declaration of triumph over death (v. 55), and Isaiah's vision of messianic joy has become a reality (Isaiah 25:6-8 = v. 54b).

Descriptive details of our risen existence remain uncertain. Human words can only approach the reality of eternal joy but then must fall silent before the mystery: Jesus lives and we shall live on with him forever.

Jesus' curriculum vitae

Dancing and the rhythmic dramatization of their religious traditions was an integral aspect of many ancient cultures. In the dance, belief takes visible form and achieves eloquent expressiveness through carefully choreographed movements. Through the dance, a spiritual heritage is passed from one generation to the next.

The Mayan peoples of Guatemala and southern Mexico still perform one such dance. A lengthy and elaborate ritual that lasts almost eight hours, the Dance of the Conquest reenacts the dying and resurrection to life of an ancient Mayan leader, Tecún Umán. As the dance unfolds, the compelling combination of music, masks and narrative surrounds both dancers and onlookers with the mystery of death and life.

Although there is no indication in scripture that Paul ever celebrated his faith in dance, he was nevertheless convinced that Christ's death and resurrection was a creative event that enfolds the believer in its mystery. Like a dance that melds body and spirit into one fluid movement, Jesus' dying and rising is the pattern that both defines and challenges the life of the believer. All that has happened for Jesus ("the one who raised the Lord Jesus") will happen also for the person who believes in him and follows his lead ("will raise us also with Jesus," v. 14).

Part of a longer section (2 Corinthians 2:14—7:4, 10:1—13:10) of his Corinthian correspondence in which Paul defended both his ministry and his apostolic calling, this short pericope grounds his claim to authenticity in the fact that he is *identified* with Christ. Elsewhere in his letters, Paul described his oneness with Christ in terms of being "in Christ" and as "I live, no longer I, but Christ lives in me" (Galatians 2:20). So complete was Paul's identification with Jesus Christ that he could tell the Corinthians that he was carrying about in his "body the dying of Jesus, so that the life of Jesus may also be manifested" in his body (2 Corinthians 4:10).

While Paul regarded the sufferings he endured for the gospel as a validation of his apostleship, his detractors in Corinth interpreted his difficulties, both personal and professional, as a contradiction to his authority. But because he was completely immersed in the saving mystery of Christ's passion, death and resurrection, Paul could not conceive of a life for himself which did *not* entail suffering. As Victor Furnish has noted, the *"curriculum vitae Pauli* was essentially the *curriculum mortis et vitae Iesu."* To put it another way, Jesus—as Lord of the Dance of Conquest—had set the tempo; as a faithful disciple, Paul lived his life in harmony with his Lord.

Paul's conviction concerning the value of suffering as a witness to the gospel and as means of identification with Christ had been bolstered by a recent near-death experience (2 Corinthians 1:8-11) of which his readers were apparently aware. This experience, as well as the daily deterioration of his aging body (v. 16), made Paul poignantly aware of his dependence on God and on his grace (v. 15). He also understood that his "inner self" was undergoing a daily growth and renewal just as his "outer self" seemed to become more decrepit. Comparing his life on earth as a temporary sojourn in an "earthly tent" (body) which was subject to affliction, Paul looked forward in hope for a transformation unto glory in eternity. Of this he had no doubt: All that God had accomplished in Jesus (viz., raising him from death to life and glory in his presence), God would also do for Paul, faithful apostle of Christ.

All who suffer sickness and pain are daily confronted with the fragility of human existence. Each day, with its share of weakness and frustration, is a little taste of death. But for those who believe, suffering becomes an opportunity to experience the power of God. Each day's weakness and pain are a passing prelude to life.

We walk by faith

By *vocation,* Paul was an apostle of Jesus Christ and minister of the good news of salvation. By *trade,* he was a tent-maker, skilled in the craft of making not only tents but also hangings, curtains and other leather goods. It was considered honorable in Paul's day for a young man to learn a trade even if he was to pursue a formal education. Rabbis, too, were encouraged to learn a trade so as to support themselves as they preached and taught their charges. A saying popular among Paul's contemporaries praised the value of work: "He who does not teach his son a trade teaches him robbery."

While he answered his call to follow Christ and to spread the gospel, there is evidence that Paul supported himself by joining the local guild and plying his trade of tentmaking (Acts 18:1-3, 1 Thessalonians 2:9, 2 Thessalonians 3:8, 1 Corinthians 4:11). Unfortunately, there were some in Corinth who doubted Paul's vocation and his message. These people were free with their criticism and probably advised Paul "not to quit his day job"! Undaunted by his detractors, Paul drew upon the symbols of his trade (tentmaker) to defend his message and his ministry for Christ.

A certain group of Corinthian Christians, influenced by gnosticism's devaluation of the body and of material existence, denigrated life in the body and the *inevitable* sufferings of the faithful believer. Although Paul admitted the *temporary* status of the body ("an earthly dwelling, a tent," v. 1), he underscored the *importance* of the body as the "place" where discipleship is learned and exercised. Just as Jesus the incarnate Son of God had effected the salvation of all peoples through his words and works and through the sufferings he endured *in his body,* thereby bringing glory to the Father, so also does the believer similarly glorify God through existence in the body.

Although Paul longed for the eschatological passage which would enable him to "go home to the Lord," he was nevertheless content and convinced that his time "away from the Lord" (or in his body) had purpose and meaning. Earlier in his first letter to the Corinthians, he had explained that the body of the Christian is a temple and dwelling place of the Spirit (1 Corinthians 3:16). As such, the faithful believer is, in the earthly and bodily existence, a *holy place* where others can meet God.

While some in Corinth accented solely the spiritual aspect of humanity and believed the actions of the body to be of no account, Paul understood that, in the end, each person would be judged "according to what he did in the body, whether good or evil" (v. 10).

The impetus which enabled Paul to face the daily difficulties of his calling with courage was his unflappable and unflagging faith. Faith empowered him with strength for his ministry and enlivened his hope for the future. At this point in his life, Paul had begun to realize that he may not be alive to welcome Jesus' second advent. Nevertheless, he had confidence that, when he died, the temporary, earthly tent of his body would be transformed by God into an eternal dwelling place.

Paul's certainty concerning the value of his physical struggle and his assurance of a future transformed existence with the Lord lend comfort and courage to every believer. The tension between our present service on earth and our longing for the full experience of eternity is made tenable by faith and by the example of faithful pioneers like Paul.

Citizens of heaven

Ancient Philippi was a proud city. First founded and called Krenides ("Little Fountains") by Greek colonists from the nearby island of Thasos, the city was soon conquered (356 BCE) by Philip II of Macedon, who renamed it after himself. The mountains overlooking the city were rich in gold and silver. The mining of these metals funded Philip's war chest and enabled him to extend his hegemony throughout most of Greece before his death in 336 BCE.

A successful military campaign in 168 BCE brought Philippi under Roman rule and the city became an important provincial outpost on the Via Egnatia which linked Rome to the Eastern world. In 42 BCE, Mark Antony and Octavian (later titled Augustus) defeated Brutus and Cassius at Philippi. Shortly thereafter, the city became a Roman colony and home to as many as 500 Roman veterans and their families. The veteran soldiers were granted Roman citizenship, and the colony enjoyed *ius italicum,* i.e., the right of proprietorship according to the Roman law and exemptions from the poll and land taxes. Expanding to include an area of more than 700 square miles, the colony of Philippi was the political, cultural and commercial center of the province of Macedonia. The citizens of Philippi were proud of their history and of the dignity and status it afforded them in the empire.

When Paul came to the city, preaching the good news of salvation, he offered the Philippians a share in a different history and a dignity far greater than any they had ever imagined. Paul reminded the proud Roman citizens of Philippi that, by faith and through the saving action of Jesus Christ, they were *citizens* of the eternal empire of *heaven.* Just as citizenship within the Roman empire conferred privileges and responsibilities upon those who enjoyed it, so also does citizenship in the kingdom of God include both blessings and challenges for its members.

Paul had already counselled the Philippians with regard to the way of life demanded by their special status in Christ. They were to so embrace the mind of Christ that they would be willing to live and die as he did. Whereas Christ did not cling to his divine status but selflessly gave of himself to the point of death, so were the Philippians called to a similar altruism for the sake of the kingdom. Because of his willingness to pour himself out in loving, caring service, Christ has been exalted and glorified by God (Philippians 2:6-11). The pattern of humiliation and exaltation evident in the life, death and resurrection of Jesus will be repeated for each Christian.

Because of their special status as citizens of heaven, believers are assured that God will work similar wonders in their lives. Included among these wonders will be the transformation of "this lowly body . . . according to the pattern of his glorified body" (v. 21). As Brendan Byrne has explained, for the Christian, "the risen Christ is exemplar as well as agent of the true humanity which God intended for human beings from the start." Elsewhere, Paul referred to the transformed, risen Lord as the "firstfruits of the Spirit" (Romans 8:23) in whose glory believers find a promise of their own.

The citizens of Philippi were proud to belong to an empire which commanded their allegiance through force and by might. The citizens of heaven are blessed to belong to a kingdom whose Lord has pledged his allegiance to his own through love and total self-giving. Rome's empire has passed into history; the kingdom of heaven is an eternal reality.

Wait and hope

Statisticians have determined that, in the average life-span of 70 years, a person spends approximately 20 years working, 20 years sleeping, six years eating, five years dressing, one year on the telephone, seven years relaxing and, among a few other activities, at least three years *waiting* for someone. While most people today would agree that *waiting* is a necessary but often tedious allotment of one's valuable time, the earliest Christians had a completely different perspective on the issue. Waiting for the return of the Lord had become a way of life. The attitude of preparedness and eager anticipation for Jesus' second advent was a factor which shaped and influenced every other activity of the believers' daily routine. Such was the perspective of the Christians at Thessalonica whose eagerness for the Lord prompted Paul's correspondence to them.

Paul had founded the community in Thessalonica while on his second missionary journey. His enthusiastic preaching of the good news of salvation found a warm welcome at the local synagogue and, as Luke tells us in Acts (17:4), "some of them were convinced and joined Paul and Silas; so too, a great number of Greeks who were worshipers, and not a few of the prominent women." When Paul moved on from Thessalonica, he left behind a vibrant community which shared his hope for a glorious future.

At this point in its development (ca. 50-51 CE), the members of the Christian community fully expected, as did Paul, to be *alive* to receive the Lord and to share in the blessings of the parousia. Some were so eager for the endtime that they quit their jobs and abandoned their ordinary activities in order to devote themselves completely to welcoming the Lord.

Others began to experience a crisis of faith when false teachers arrived in the city, attacking Paul's authority and criticizing the gospel he had preached. These problems were exacerbated by the fact that some members of the community had died and it seemed likely that more would also pass away before the second advent of Jesus. When Timothy reported these concerns, Paul wrote quickly and lovingly to the Thessalonians to strengthen them in their faith and to encourage them in their hope.

Basing his counsel on the principle that those who live and die in Christ will also rise with him, Paul assured his readers that nothing, *not even death,* will breach the bond which unites Christ with those who believe in him. Because Christ has conquered death, those who have made this passage before his return will not be at a disadvantage; on the contrary, they shall rise first (v. 16).

Then, summoning the recognized symbols of apocalyptic literature (clouds, trumpets, angels), Paul painted for his readers a vision of their joyous reunion with the Lord Jesus. Through word and symbol, he bolstered their faith so that they would be able to meet the daily struggles, inherent in their Christian commitment, without losing heart.

"Console one another with this message," Paul advised the Thessalonians as they waited for Jesus and for the fulfillment his return would bring. Today, with the approach of the third Christian millennium, Paul's call to watchful, faithful, hopeful waiting is no less compelling and consoling.

2 TIMOTHY 2:8-13

Remember Jesus

"*R*emember Jesus . . . you can depend on this." With advice and assurances such as these, the author of 2 Timothy sought to encourage his readers to maintain themselves in the integrity of their Christian faith. First called the "pastoral epistles" by Thomas Aquinas in the 13th century, 1 and 2 Timothy and Titus are purported to be the final letters of Paul, written shortly before his death in the mid-60s CE. Most contemporary scholars agree, however, that the letters were probably written ca. 100 CE by one who wished to safeguard the gospel and to extend the heritage, insights and teachings of the apostle to a later generation. For this reason, 2 Timothy is presented as a last will and testament of Paul, offering counsel and sympathizing with the struggles of a pastor whose church was ravaged by persecution from without and by doctrinal disputes from within.

The letter was purported to be set within the context of Paul's final imprisonment in Rome. Undaunted, he declared that the messenger may be chained but the message, the word of God, is greater than its messenger. The word of God continues to speak and is as true and trustworthy as ever (v. 9). Resolutely, the author shared with his readers his conviction that his sufferings were not meaningless. Because of his solidarity with Christ, the trials and tribulations inherent in his ministry had redemptive value (v. 10). No doubt, these words lent strength and courage to those believers whose Christian values and lifestyle made them similarly vulnerable to persecution and familiar with suffering.

In an attempt to offer security to a community beset by insecurities, the author set forth for his readers: (1) a summary of the gospel, v. 8; (2) the ramifications of the

Christian life, vv. 11-12; and (3) an admonition concerning faithful discipleship, v. 13. Underscoring the three main aspects of the good news, the author reminded his readers of the incarnation (descendant of David), *death* and *resurrection* of Jesus. Remember this, he exclaimed! This had been the gospel preached by the apostles and by Paul. Regardless of the changing circumstances of their lives, this same gospel was to be preserved intact and undiluted for all ages.

Quoting an early Christian hymn (vv. 11-12a), the author recalled Jesus' passage from death to life. This same passage is to be reflected in the life of the faithful believer in two ways. First, in baptism, the Christian dies to sin and death so as to rise to new life, forgiveness and reconciliation in Christ (see also Romans 6:4, 8). Second, the believer who is called to the ultimate witness of martyrdom for the faith will also pass from death to life in Christ. Those who do not deny the gospel but who "hold out to the end" are assured of a share in Christ's glory (v. 12a). By the time this letter was written, all of the apostolic eyewitnesses to Jesus and many other faithful believers had made the double passage from death to life with Christ—first in baptism and then in martyrdom.

A somber warning concludes this pericope. Those who deny Christ deny also the passage through death to life whereby Christ defined his role in the mystery of salvation. One of the most wondrous and yet frightening aspects of human existence is the gift of freedom which enables each person to choose or to reject God's overtures of saving love. As Paul Wrightman explains, "Jesus will respect what we have chosen to do with our human freedom. To force himself upon us would be to deny himself because it is his nature to honor our choice. He remains forever faithful in the sense that he does everything in his power—with the exception of force—to assure our salvation."

"Remember Jesus" who has made the passage from death to life. Baptized believers are incorporated into the process of that passage. Suffering, struggling believers are called daily to renew their solidarity with his dying so as to experience the joy

and glory of his rising. "Remember Jesus" and your passage is assured. "You can depend on this."

We shall be like him!

*I*n the years before her death in 1993, actress Audrey Hepburn devoted her time and energies to bettering the living conditions of the disadvantaged children of the world. Her own childhood had been marred by the ravages of war; she had known hunger, fear and the loss of family and home. Determined to do what she could to ease the plight and restore the dignity of children in need, she joined UNICEF and traveled thousands of miles around the world. Those who witnessed Miss Hepburn's gentle demeanor with the children could not help but be moved by her reverence for their fragile, precious lives.

Her work and the work of others like her implore the world to be responsible for the well-being of its children. As members of the human community, the children of the world deserve a share in the same dignity, rights and privileges enjoyed by adult members. When the presbyter who authored 1 John wrote to one of the house churches in Ephesus, he addressed his readers as *children of God* and reminded them of the dignity, rights and privileges inherent in that special status.

In words reminiscent of the gospel around which the Johannine community developed (viz., John 3:16), the presbyter marveled at the gratuitous and beneficent love of God (v. 1). As William Barclay has explained, by *nature* we are *creatures* of God, but through *love* and by *grace* we become God's *children.*

There are two words in English which aptly illustrate this difference: *paternity* and *fatherhood.* Through paternity, a person is responsible for the physical existence of a child; but fatherhood creates a relationship in which a child is *willingly* embraced. Embraced also are the blessings and responsibilities for loving, caring, nurturing, defending and guiding the child through life. In paternity, there is a *legal* obligation; in fatherhood, obligations are met with *love* that is faithfully and selflessly bestowed. Paternity does not necessarily admit a child to family life but fatherhood involves relatedness to a whole host of family members (brothers, sisters, etc.).

Christians are loved and claimed as children by God the Father and redeemed by the saving love of their brother Jesus. They are called to live lives worthy of their blessings or, as Raymond Brown has expressed it, "with salvific relevance." Consecrated as children by God's love, they become sharers in the familial love of the Father and the Son. As such, they do not belong to the world and are rejected by the world, as was Jesus (v. 1 = John 15:18-19, 17:14-16). Like their brother who has already made the passage from death to glory, believers in Jesus will enjoy a future of eternal life (v. 2 = John 17:24).

Describing the future of the believer in terms of being "like him" and seeing "him as he is," the presbyter brought his readers "full circle," to a consideration of God's creation of humanity. Made in the "image and likeness of God" (Genesis 1:26), it remains the goal and purpose of each human person to become all that God has intended. Inasmuch as the believer conforms his/her life and all its moments to the person and mission of Jesus Christ, that likeness becomes more and more evident. In the end, God will recognize and bless his faithful children with the same glory enjoyed by the Son, and the joy of seeing him face to face will be ours.

The words of the presbyter encourage his readers to live, here and now, as God's children, faithful to the privileges, responsibilities and dignity which our special status entails. He also offers the hope of an eternal "family reunion" for all who remain true to the love of the Father as loyal brothers and sisters of the Son.

Love laid down his life

When Martin Luther King, Jr., died in 1968, he left behind a legacy of wisdom, tolerance and patient endurance to all who are concerned for civil rights. Although he is best remembered for his political influence and accomplishments, he also served with his father as a devoted and competent associate pastor of a church in Atlanta, Georgia. An admirer of the zeal of the early believers in Jesus, Dr. King once wrote in a letter, "In those days, the church was not merely a thermometer that recorded the ideas and principles of a popular belief; it was a thermostat that transformed the mores of society."

When the presbyter-author of 1 John wrote a letter to one of the house churches in Ephesus, he for his part expressed a similar conviction, viz., the challenge of those who believe in Christ requires a daily translation of their faith into a palpable and practical love for others.

From what can be deduced from the Johannine letters, the community which sprung from the rich heritage of the fourth gospel was divided over certain key issues. Eventually, the community split, with the secessionists claiming superior knowledge of God and special intimacy with him, while denying the true humanity of Jesus and any obligation with regard to ethical living. Due to a distorted interpretation of the fourth gospel's concept of realized eschatology, the Johannine schismatics claimed that they had already attained the absolute *fullness* of eternal life.

Confronting his adversaries in the midst of their own argument, the presbyter asserted that such a passage "from death to life" (v. 14) should be self-evident in the lives of those who had experienced it. Like Jesus, in whom the passage from death to life was made possible, the life of a believer should be characterized by love. Love of others is the criterion of life in Christ; love for others is the measure of true knowledge of God. If this criterion were not met, then there has been no real passage—there is no life. Indeed, charged the presbyter, those who refuse to love their brothers and sisters are murderers.

Earlier in his letter, the author of 1 John attributed Cain's evil deed to a lack of love. Because he did not allow God's gift of love to fill his life and permeate his words and works, Cain opened himself to the bitter corruption of hatred; and hatred led to murder (1 John 3:12). In words reminiscent of those attributed to Jesus in the gospels (John 8:44, Matthew 5:21-22), the presbyter warned his readers that the hatred which leads to murder precludes any share in eternal life.

Lest we too easily dismiss ourselves from culpability in the regard, Raymond E. Brown has explained that the reference to murder should also be understood as hyperbole for maltreatment. While most Christians will never commit outright murder, few of us can claim that we have never mistreated another. Such maltreatment would include words and works which have been *committed* against another, as well as those words and works which could have benefited another but were *omitted* or withheld.

As a final clarification of the extent and quality of love which should characterize the life of the believer, the presbyter reminded his readers that they had come to *know* love in the person and mission of Jesus Christ: "He laid down his life for us" (v. 16a). As William Barclay has explained, Jesus literally gave his life; but, for most of us, life will not end so tragically. However, the same principle of conduct should govern our lives. To lay down one's life involves a willingness to surrender that which has value in our life so as to enrich the life of another. To live and love in this way is to participate in Jesus' passage from death to life and to know the happiness of eternal life.

*T*hose who eulogize someone who has died rarely speak of the *wealth they had accumulated or the degrees they had earned. Little mention is made of power and prestige because these are* *not the true measure of a person. The only true measure of a person's life is the immeasurable quality of their love.*

Dying in the Lord

Each of us has memories, a personal "root cellar" of mental and emotional treasures which, in their turn, can occupy a moment in our consciousness and carry us to a different time and place. One of my most vivid religious memories is of a homily preached by a visiting priest. As a child of eight, I had never considered the topic he put before us that day: death. The priest explained that, each day we live, we also do a little dying. Each day that passes brings us closer to that final moment we call "death." The words I heard that day engraved themselves upon my memory and have come back to speak to me many times.

When the author of Revelation wrote to encourage his persecuted friends in their daily struggle with living and dying, he also wished to strengthen in them a vivid recollection of the good news of Jesus, dead and risen. As fellow members of the Johannine community, the author and his readers inherited a memory of Jesus who had invited his disciples to "remain in me as I *remain* in you" (John 15:4).

"Remain" (in Greek, *menein*) can also mean "abide," "stay" or "dwell." This term occurs 68 times in the Johannine literature (gospel; 1, 2 and 3 John; Revelation) and expresses the enduring union of the Father with the Son, and of the Son with the believer. One with Jesus during life, the faithful believer is also one with the dying of Jesus. In other words, those who daily remain *in Jesus*, despite all the factors which militate against that union (viz., persecution, doubt, delayed eschatology, etc.), will also be privileged to make the final passage through death to life *with him*.

In order to underscore the importance of such enduring and faithful union, the seer-author of Revelation was told, "Write this down!" The ensuing beatitude pronounced joy and blessing on those who remain in Jesus even to—and through— the point of death: "Happy are the dead who die in the Lord!" As a result of their daily living and dying in Christ, the faithful are assured that they shall find *rest*. For most human beings, "rest" is a term which describes the interval between one task and the next. Indeed, this notion appears in the Christian scriptures (e.g., Mark 6:31, 14:41; Luke 12:19). But the scriptures also reveal a notion of rest as the renewal of the inner person (1 Corinthians 16:18; 2 Corinthians 7:13; Philemon 7, 20). In this verse from Revelation, *rest* means the eschatological fulfillment of the redeemed. Paul offered a similar hope of rest to those who endured suffering for the sake of Christ in this life (2 Thessalonians 1:7). He further explained that the eschatological rest of the faithful was equivalent to: (1) union with Christ, 1 Thessalonians 4:17; (2) participation in the kingdom, 2 Thessalonians 1:5; and (3) a share in the glory bestowed upon Jesus himself, 2 Thessalonians 1:12.

The reference to good works does not imply that the cherished rest of the faithful is anything but a gratuitous gift of God. Elsewhere, in his letter to the Ephesians and Thyatirans, the author described "works" in terms of "endurance" (Revelation 2:2) and "love, faith and service" (Revelation 2:19). Such qualities are a vital and necessary expression of the faith of the committed believer. These are not a list of merits which can be weighed or numbered but an integral aspect of the disciple's character.

As William Barclay has explained, "When you leave this earth, all you can take with you is yourself. If you come to the end of your life still one with Christ, you will take with you a character, tried and tested like gold, which has something of his reflection in it; if you take with you to the world beyond a character like that, blessed are you!"

In the daily dying which is consonant with life in Christ, believers prepare for their final passage to life, to rest, to happiness. "Write this down."

A new creation

---

*I*n the same year that Sir Thomas More coined the term "utopia" to refer to an ideal commonwealth wherein harmony reigns because of mutually beneficent institutions, Machiavelli wrote *The Prince* which propounds a political doctrine that denies the relevance of morality while asserting that treachery and deceit are justified in the pursuit and maintenance of political power. The year was 1516, and the situation was no doubt made more precarious by the fact that firearms were first manufactured in France in that year.

In the ever changing ebb and flow of human history, the ambitions of tyrants have been countered (but not always balanced) by the hopes of humanity for a better existence. Plato was perhaps the first literary architect of an ideal world, recording his ideas in *The Republic*. Aldous Huxley wrote of a *Brave New World* (1932) while Henry D. Thoreau idealized and immortalized Walden Pond in his *Walden*. Pope John XXIII promulgated *Pacem in terris* in the wake of the 1962 Cuban missile crisis which threatened the world with nuclear holocaust. President Lyndon B. Johnson wished to create the "Great Society" despite the vitiating effects of the war in Vietnam.

But when the author of Revelation, in his turn, observed the political and moral climate of the Roman empire and witnessed the ravages which Roman tyranny was wreaking upon the growing church, he offered a *unique* solution to the situation. Rather than propose a merely human societal reform (however ethical and ideal it may be), the seer shared with his contemporaries a vision of *divine* intervention.

Like the earlier series of visions concerning the future of the world and the climax of salvation history (Revelation 4:1— 5:14), this vision features a large white throne from which the sovereign God of all creation renders the universal and final judgment (v. 11). It is interesting that human representations of "Justice" portray a blindfolded figure as a sign of the impartiality with which justice is impersonally meted out to all. But in the scriptures, wherein "justice" means righteousness, the just God *sees* and *knows* and *judges* each one *personally* according to the absolute truth of his loving and saving will for humanity.

As all the dead from every age are gathered into the divine presence, two books reveal the status of their lives. In the scroll or book of life (vv. 12, 15) and in the scroll or book of deeds (v. 12), the personal history of each life is recorded. These deeds testify for and/or against each person, pronouncing guilt or innocence. Eduard Shick observes: "Election and works, grace and cooperation, calling and its personal fulfillment must tally if the judgment is to be positive. The final judgment, therefore, is naught but the universal disclosure of the decision everybody has (already) made for himself." Karl Rahner has further elucidated: "The individual who is finally saved by God's grace alone (which is what theology means by saying that human beings must be transformed by the 'light of glory' in order to be capable of heaven) remains conditioned by what he has done and what he has become in history."

Once each person's life choices have been disclosed, the judgment is pronounced and retribution ensues. All those whose choices have absolutely negated life experience death and its finality forever. Destroyed also are death and Hades (Sheol, abode of the dead). But for those whose daily struggle has been characterized by cooperation with God's saving grace, there shall be a new and wondrous existence. Just like the first creation, these new heavens and new earth will be the product of divine intervention. Because the author of justice now reigns sovereign on the throne, there shall be no place for evil in the new creation. This fact is borne out in the abolishment of the sea. Popularly believed to be the source of evil and chaos, the elimination of the sea therefore underscored the elemental message of the book of Revelation, viz., the triumph of goodness over evil and of life over death.

Rather than live in fear of an unknown future, the believer has a lifetime to create a personal history of faithful responses to the loving overtures of a just and gracious God.

All things new

"*I* shall be with you," "You shall be my people, and I will be your God"—promises of presence like these weave a visible tapestry of loving care and relatedness throughout both the Hebrew and Christian scriptures. Such a promise was made to Abraham, ancestral father in faith of all believers (Genesis 17:4-8). Moses was bolstered for his mission by numerous affirmations of divine accompaniment (Exodus 3:12, 6:7, etc.). A similar promise assured the dynasty of David (1 Samuel 16:18, 18:12, 18:14, 18:28, 20:13; 2 Samuel 5:10, 7:3, 7:9, 7:14). Pledges of divine presence empowered Israel's judges with courage (Judges 6:12-13, 6:16, 2:18) and the prophets with strength (Jeremiah 1:8, 19; 15:20; 20:11).

And despite its less than perfect record of fidelity, the nation of Israel received repeated assurances of God's unwavering companionship with his people (Numbers 14:9; 2 Chronicles 20:17; Haggai 1:13, 2:4; Ezekiel 34:30; Isaiah 43:2, 45:14, 41:10; Jeremiah 42:11, 46:28). The promise of God dwelling in their midst was tantamount to a pledge of life and salvation for his people (Leviticus 26:11-12, Jeremiah 31:33, Ezekiel 37:27, Isaiah 7:14).

This promise of presence and relatedness was brought to its ultimate fulfillment in the person and mission of Jesus Christ. In Jesus, the divine presence has become visible and tangible through the very medium of human existence (John 1:14). Given this wonderful history of divine attendance, it is not surprising that visions of the future life should be similarly portrayed. As this reading from Revelation reveals, the focal point of the heavenly Jerusalem is none other than God's ever-abiding, lifegiving presence.

With this vision of the new creation, the biblical story has come full circle. Just as the Genesis author described the first creation as being brought forth by the power of God's word ("Let there be," Genesis 1:3), so also is the new creation invoked by a divine command ("I make all things new," v. 5). And just as the first creation was intended to be a place of joy and peace, so also is the new creation to be characterized by the abolishment of tears, pain, death and mourning.

No doubt this vision was a source of strength and encouragement for the author's contemporaries. The earthly Jerusalem had been destroyed by Roman troops in 70 CE, and the ensuing years of persecution had made tears and pain a reality in the life of every believer. The image of the new Jerusalem adorned as a bride for her husband was a symbol of the eschatological union of the faithful with God. This image is made more poignant by the fact that Rome (Babylon) had been earlier portrayed as a harlot who spawned murderers, liars and idolaters (Revelation 17). In sharp contrast, the new Jerusalem is the legitimate and covenanted bride, mother to those whom God calls "son" (v. 7).

"Without cost" (v. 6), the faithful sons and daughters of God will slake their thirst with the water of life. A symbol of the messianic era in the Hebrew scriptures (Isaiah 12:3, 41:18, 44:3-4, 55:1, Ezekiel 47:1), the water of life signified the gift of the Spirit for Christians (John 4:10-14, 7:38-39). In this vision of watery abundance, the hopes of both testaments meet and are fulfilled by the one seated on the throne.

With a claim earlier attributed to the risen Christ (Revelation 1:8), the enthroned one claims to be Alpha and Omega, Beginning and End. Alpha and Omega are the first and last letters of the Greek alphabet. The title, "first and last," reprises the prophetic pronouncement of Israel's monotheistic faith, a faith that evolved only after centuries of dallying with false gods (Isaiah 44:6). In the new creation, the struggle of the faithful is blessed with the presence of the one, true God.

"Beginning" (in Greek, *arche*) means first, not simply in reference to time but also in the sense of the *source* of all. "End" (in Greek, *telos*) connotes not just the last moment in time but the *goal* for which all is intended. In other words, the joy of the faithful in the new creation is to live forever in the presence of the one who is both the source and goal of all existence.

The life of every believer is supported by numerous and varied experiences of the divine presence. These experiences sustain us in the daily struggle to believe until that moment when faith becomes unnecessary and the passage of time is replaced by the eternal now.

Gospel

MATTHEW 5:1-12

Carpe diem

---

*R*egardless of whether he is accepted in faith or not, Jesus of Nazareth is undisputedly the most important figure in all of human history. More than anyone who has ever lived, he has influenced the thoughts, values, ideals and lifestyles of humankind for almost two millennia. None of the Caesars, for all their power, held such sway; not Confucius or Alexander, not Hitler or Charlemagne—no other living person has left such a legacy. Part of that legacy, albeit one of the least understood aspects, is contained in this excerpt from the gospel according to Matthew.

Known as the "beatitudes" because of the term ("blest," Latin *beatus*) with which each statement is introduced, this collection of sayings has for too long been regarded by too many as a message of solace for those who have been "shortchanged" by the world. Some look upon the promises contained in the beatitudes as a sort of "consolation prize," intended to motivate the pious "losers" in this life to "grin and bear it" because there will be "pie-in-the-sky when you die." Cliches notwithstanding, nothing could be farther from the truth.

Far from being a collection of pious platitudes, the beatitudes are an authoritative, bold and frontal challenge which demands that each person examine his/her way of thinking, choosing and living. Key to any understanding of this challenge is an accurate appreciation of the term "blest."

In Hebrew, the word is *'ashre*; in Greek, it is rendered *makarios*. In both languages, the word "blest" refers not to some *future* bliss in another world or in an afterlife; rather, the term is an affirmation of a *present* and ever-evolving happiness which finds its source in God himself. As Earl F. Palmer has explained, this biblical notion of happiness and blessedness "has to do with orientation, perspective, [and] the discovery of what is meaningful in the midst of shallow, superficial options." The person who finds blessedness has discovered the right path of relatedness to God despite the manipulations and detours of a hostile environment.

Foremost among those pronounced blest are the poor in spirit. These have "renounced all preconceived opinions in the wholehearted search for God." To be poor in this sense is "to be willing to set aside present habits of thought, present views and prejudices, a present way of life if necessary." It is, in fact, "to jettison anything and everything that can stand in the way of finding God" (quotes from Emmet Fox). The poor are pronounced blest in that the reign of God *is* theirs. Note the present tense. The reign of God is both a *present* experience and a *future* promise.

Like all the other beatitudes, this first one is a proclamation of the salvation that has become available to all in the person and mission of Jesus Christ. But this is not a salvation which falls from the sky like a warm blanket, securely enfolding all it touches. This salvation is "a treasure hidden in a field" which is recognized and retrieved only by the lowly and the sorrowing, the hungry and the thirsty. Moreover, it is also "a pearl of great price" which can be claimed only by the merciful, the singlehearted, the peacemakers and the persecuted.

Those who grasp the message of the beatitudes do not simply engage themselves in a program of preparation for *future* joys. On the contrary, the beatitudes extend an existential challenge to every believer, summed up in the Roman poet Horace's admonition, *Carpe diem* ("Seize the day").

Live this *day so completely committed to Christ that* his *goodness is reflected in* your *eyes and* his *kindness is felt through* your *hands. Live this day so completely conformed to* his *mind and heart that those who see and hear* you *will know* his *mercy and experience* his *love. Seize* this *day and eternity is already in your grasp.*

Come to me

One of the most memorable scenes from the musical *Fiddler on the Roof* is that of Tevya booming out the song, "Tradition." "Here in Anatevka," he explains, "we have traditions for everything . . . how to eat, how to sleep, how to work, even how to wear clothes . . . . How did it begin? No one knows! But because of our traditions, everyone knows who he is and what God expects him to do!"

The earthly character Tevya appealed to tradition as the reason why things did *not* and should *not* change ("Tradition is how we keep our balance"). Jesus appealed to tradition as a motivation for *radical* change. With the words, "Everything has been handed over to me by my Father" (v. 27), Jesus identified himself as the unique tradition of the Father. "Handing over" (in Greek, *paradosis*) was a technical term which referred to the process of preserving and giving over or passing on a body of truths, beliefs and practices. Christians later referred to this "tradition" as the "deposit of faith."

For the Jews, tradition consisted in the handing over, from one generation to the next, of their understanding of the Torah or law with all its precepts. The law was central to Israel's faith and was considered to be a major source of revelation and the means by which God manifested his covenant relationship with his people. In this particular pericope, however, Matthew has portrayed *Jesus* as *the* source of revelation and *the* means by which believers can come to know and enter into relationship with the Father: "No one knows the Father but the Son and anyone to whom the Son wishes to reveal him" (v. 27b).

In his prayer of thanksgiving for the revelation of the Father manifested through him (vv. 25-26), Jesus alluded to the fact that his teachings had been a cause of crisis among those who had heard him. In Greek, the word *krisis* means "decision" or "judgment." Those confronted with the words and works of Jesus were thereby impelled to *decide* for him or against him. Those who rejected him brought upon themselves a negative *judgment*. Those who opted in faith *for* Jesus were gifted with knowledge of the Father and all the blessings that entailed. In this Matthean text, those who found themselves on either side of the crisis posed by Jesus were "the learned and the clever" and "the merest children."

Those who were schooled in the law (scribes, priests) and those who were known for their meticulous legal observance (Pharisees) were challenged by Jesus. His authoritative and innovative interpretation of the law (Matthew 5:21-48) summoned them to move beyond the letter of the law to consider the spirit of the one to whom the law was attributed. Such a change of mind and heart required a radical readjustment of attitude: "The learned and the clever" had to become as wise as "merest children."

Once this adjustment or conversion was begun, then Jesus' invitation to discipleship (vv. 28-30) could be recognized and accepted. With words reminiscent of Israel's rich sapiential heritage, Jesus is depicted as Wisdom personified. In that capacity, he: (1) shares the same nature as the Father, Wisdom 7:22-26; (2) reveals the Father, Wisdom 8:3-4 and 9:9-18, Proverbs 8:22-36; and (3) gives rest to all who come to him, Sirach 6:28 and 51:23-27. A caring and giving mentor, Jesus promises that the yoke of those who accept discipleship will be light. Compared to the burden of the law which the scribes and the Pharisees multiplied exponentially and imposed (Matthew 23:4), Jesus' yoke is made "easy" by the love with which he welcomes and supports each child of the Father.

*A*s *believers in Jesus who uniquely knows and reveals the Father, we have become sharers in a tradition which gives life. Because of Jesus, "everyone knows who he is and what God expects us to do."*

MATTHEW 25:1-13

The boss may come today

On one of his several expeditions to the Antarctic, Sir Ernest Shackleton (1874-1922) and his crew were shipwrecked off Caird coast. Adrift for ten months, their ship, the *Endurance,* was eventually crushed in the pack ice, and its crew was forced to cling to ice floes for the next five months until they could scramble ashore on Elephant Island.

From there, Shackleton and five of his party sailed 800 miles to find help in rescuing the rest of their stranded crew. Only after several months and four relief expeditions was Shackleton successful in digging a channel through the now frozen ice to rescue his men. Not only were the crew members alive and well, but they were all ready to board the rescue ship as soon as it moored.

Once they were safely aboard and homeward bound, Shackleton questioned his men concerning their amazing state of preparedness despite so many months of waiting. Each morning, they told him, their leader would roll up his sleeping bag and instruct the others to do the same: "Get your things ready, boys, the boss may come today!" This eager expectation, as well as the hope and optimism concomitant with such an attitude of readiness, did much to ensure the well-being and survival of Shackleton's crew. The parable of the ten bridesmaids was intended to serve a similar purpose.

Peculiar to Matthew, this parable is part of a series of parables which constitute the fifth and final discourse of the gospel. Eschatological in tone, the message of the parable underwent considerable development as it was accommodated by the ever-growing and evolving Christian community. At its basic or primary level, the parable reprised familiar Old Testament nuptial imagery to describe the relationship between God and his people. Yahweh is the bridegroom and Israel (or the new Israel, the church) is to remain faithful and attentive to receive him. In Jesus' day, the parable challenged his contemporaries to recognize the fact that the divine visitation of the bridegroom had been realized in his person and through his mission.

By the time the parable was written down and incorporated into Matthew's gospel in the 80s CE, it functioned as a call to vigilance and preparation for Jesus' *second* appearance. As such, it served a pedagogical purpose, instructing all would-be disciples (v. 1) concerning the importance of enduring faith as well as the translation of that faith into authentic service.

Take note that the *only* difference among the ten bridesmaids is the fact that some brought oil with them for their torches whereas others did not. *All* had torches, *all* experienced his delay, *all* nodded off to sleep, *all* were roused at midnight by the same cry. But those who had thought to bring oil with them were described as sensible and were welcomed to participate in the feasting when the bridegroom appeared. Those with no oil found themselves barred from the celebration. They were called foolish and were not acknowledged by the bridegroom despite their desperate, last minute maneuvering to equip themselves with oil.

Key to understanding the significance of the oil and its importance for disciples is a reference which occurs earlier in the Matthean gospel. Explaining the distinction between those who will experience salvation and those who will not, Jesus is quoted as saying, "Not everyone who says to me, 'Lord, Lord,' will enter the kingdom of heaven, but only the one who does the will of my Father in heaven" (Matthew 7:21).

The wise bridesmaids represent those disciples whose lives have been characterized by personal and enduring commitment to the will of the Father; this is the "oil" that has lit the lamp of their faith and has kept them prepared to recognize and receive Jesus in all of his advents. Because this oil represents a relationship of faith and service that has been carefully cultivated and tended, it cannot be borrowed from another or hastily scraped together at the last minute.

*E*ach day that we awake and find ourselves alive, we have been given yet another opportunity to tend the lamp of our faith and the light of our good works (Matthew 5:16). Those who are wise will avail themselves of each day's opportunities. They will listen wisely and respond fully when they hear the word: "Get your things ready, boys, the boss may come today!"

Come, inherit the kingdom

*E*very culture within the vast and varied throng of human societies has developed its own criteria for categorizing and/or separating its members. The ancient Romans ascribed to a system which differentiated between the aristocratic patricians and the more numerous but less influential plebeian class. Ancient Greeks were often classified by the philosophy according to which they lived. A complex order of highly restrictive castes developed in the seventh century BCE is still operative in India today. Closer to home, people are distinguished according to gender, race and age.

Data-collecting surveys further classify people according to their marital status, the level of their education, the salary they earn and the cost of their homes. Students are tested and grouped according to their measured abilities. Employees are evaluated periodically, and their rating determines salary, advancement and security benefits. Military personnel are differentiated by rank, years of service and the number of campaigns in which they have participated.

In a word, human beings are accustomed to the variety of factors, both authentic and artificial, which earmark us as similar to or different from one another. In this gospel text (unique to the Matthean gospel), the linchpin is also a criterion of separation. But what *is* the criterion?

The scene is an eschatological one. The Son of Man, enthroned in glory, is rendering judgment upon all the nations. Those who are judged favorably are blessed to inherit the kingdom (v. 1). For those upon whom judgment falls harshly, there is the curse of everlasting separation from the Father and the Son (v. 41).

At first glance, it may appear that the specific deeds of mercy (giving food to the hungry, drink to the thirsty, clothing to the naked, etc.) constitute the criterion whereby humankind will be judged. It may also appear that this pericope is but another parable (albeit a striking one) among the many parables in Matthew's gospel. But, as John Meier has so aptly explained, this text is not a parable but the "unveiling of the truth which lay behind all the parables" in Matthew's eschatological discourse (chapters 24-25).

Moreover, it is not the deeds or works *in themselves* which are the criteria for judgment but the fact that the judge claims that these deeds have been done *to him*. The Son of Man is indeed Emmanuel, God-with-us. He has become fully incarnate and has completely identified himself with the poor, the hungry, the outcast, the oppressed. Notice the fact that the Son of Man insists, "*I* was hungry . . . *I* was thirsty . . . *I* was a stranger . . . *I* was ill . . . and you gave *me*. . . ."

Therefore, the judgment to be rendered upon all nations shall find its basis not simply in ethics but in *christology*. Jesus is the criterion of judgment as well as the judge. The deeds done for others factor into the final evaluation for humanity because they help to define each believer's essential response to and relationship with the judge. To neglect these kindnesses is to negate not only one's fellow human beings but also Jesus himself.

In its literature concerning aid programs, the World Council of Churches warns against misinterpreting this gospel simply as a call to provide for the *material* needs of the world's poor. Jesus did not advocate merely doling out aid. He called for a personal investment in the poor and the needy for *his* sake. Early in Matthew's gospel, Jesus had similarly charged his disciples: "Everyone who acknowledges me before others, I will acknowledge before my heavenly Father. But whoever denies me before others, I will deny before my heavenly Father" (Matthew 10:32-33).

All of life is an opportunity for acknowledging Christ. Each day, the believer is challenged to seek Jesus and to find him in the hungry, the poor, the sick and the imprisoned with whom he has chosen to identify. This continuing acknowledgment and this daily search will have eternal consequences.

He has arrived!

*A*mong the Yoruba, a tribe indigenous to Nigeria, those who have died are never referred to as having *departed*. Because of their firm belief in the continuation and amelioration of life after death, the Yoruba joyfully proclaim of their dead, "They have *arrived!*" Death is regarded as a journey, and the elderly anticipate its passage by declaring, "I am going *home!*"

In Mark's gospel, the death of Jesus is a focal event of paramount importance. Until that moment in the passion narrative, the true identity of Jesus has been either misunderstood and/or muffled in secrecy. But in the very act of dying, Jesus is fully and definitively revealed. In death, Jesus has indeed *arrived* and, through his *homecoming*, he has opened the way to the Father for all believers.

Mark accented the climactic character of Jesus' death with a number of vivid details. The darkness which covered the earth from noon until midafternoon could be variously explained as the result of some naturally occurring phenomenon, e.g., an eclipse, a sandstorm, etc. But more importantly, the darkness recalled the prophetic warnings about the Day of the Lord. From the time of Amos, that day was regarded as a time of great judgment when God would wage war on sin in order to reestablish his covenant with the repentant (Amos 5:18, 5:20, 8:9; Joel 2).

As Henry Wansbrough has noted, the darkness at the time of the crucifixion "sets the stage for understanding Jesus' death as the decisive saving event which forever decided between goodness and evil and underscored the means by which the battle could be waged."

Just as the death of Jesus annulled the power of sin and evil, so also did his dying abrogate the traditional means whereby believers approached and recognized God. Mark signals this abrogation by telling his readers that, at the moment of Jesus' death, the temple curtain was rent from top to bottom. The curtain in question veiled the Holy of Holies, the most sacred place in the temple. It was here that Yahweh was believed to be especially present to his people. No one entered the Holy of Holies except the high priest who did so only once a year on the Day of Atonement.

The torn temple curtain signified the fact that, through Jesus' death, access to God was no longer restricted. The Holy of Holies which had formerly been hidden from the people would be replaced by Jesus himself, in whom and through whom all peoples could draw near and openly experience the loving, merciful presence of God.

Although misunderstood by those who heard him, Jesus' cry from the cross (*"Eloi, Eloi,"* v. 34) also underscored the salvific character of his death. Some have suggested that this cry reveals the depth of Jesus' suffering as he allowed himself to be completely vulnerable to the ravages of sin and its effects. But others have understood Jesus' cry as the beginning words of Psalm 22, a prayer of confident trust in God during a time of affliction. The psalm concludes with the triumphant declaration of deliverance and justification for the one who has suffered as well as for his brethren (Psalm 22:25-32).

Significantly, the evangelist waited until the moment of Jesus' saving and liberating death to openly reveal his identity: "Clearly, this man was the Son of God" (v. 39). The centurion's declaration was further ratified by the scene at Jesus' tomb. Functioning as an *angelus interpres*, the young man explained the meaning of the empty tomb: "Jesus of Nazareth, the one who was crucified, is risen!"

*N*o longer among the dead, Jesus has arrived. His saving mission accomplished, he has gone home to the Father. Because of Jesus, the harsh reality of each believer's death is not only a departure—it is also an arrival, a homecoming.

God has visited his people

When the fourth century CE Spanish pilgrim, Egeria, travelled to the Holy Land, she visited the house church at Naim which was believed to be the home of the widow whose son was raised to life by Jesus. Archaeologists from the University of Florida confirmed the authenticity of the site in 1982. This same team of experts unearthed the circular wall which surrounded the city, the gate of which was the place where Jesus met the widow and her son's funeral cortege (v. 11). Today the site is identified with the Muslim town of Nein about eight miles southeast of Nazareth.

A touching narrative replete with the gamut of human emotions, the resuscitation of the widow's son demonstrates Jesus' power to save and to liberate. This event also provides a concrete illustration of the answer Jesus would soon give to the disciples of John the Baptizer. When sent by John to ask, "Are you the one who is to come, or should we look for another?" the messengers were told, "Go and tell John . . . the blind regain their sight, the lame walk, lepers are cleansed, the deaf hear, *the dead are raised,* the poor have the good news preached to them" (Luke 7:20-22). These deeds, which had been traditionally associated with the messianic restoration of Israel (Isaiah 35:5-6, 58:6, 61:1-2), were claimed by Jesus as his own during the statement with which he officially inaugurated his public mission (Luke 4:16-21).

Throughout his ministry, Jesus' special predilection for the poor, the sick and the sinner was authentically reflective of the mind and heart of God. Nevertheless, this practice set Jesus at odds with many of his contemporaries who regarded such persons as steeped in sin, cursed by God and therefore deserving of their sad lot in life. Jesus was charged with "misleading the people" and "inciting the people to revolt" (Luke 23:2, 14) because he was not "politically correct." In other words, Jesus violated the status quo which, on the grounds of religious purity, restricted persons, places, things and events as clean or unclean.

In clear violation of the accepted religious and cultural mores of his day which regarded the habitually unclean as unredeemable, Jesus freely and often associated with these outcasts, thereby redrawing the parameters of salvation. Each association of Jesus with the "unclean" resulted in their being healed, made whole and restored to the life of the community.

In this particular narrative, Jesus did not allow the laws of ritual purity concerning corpses (Numbers 19:11, 16) to deter him. He reached into the "unclean" realm of death, broke the barriers which separated the son from his mother, restored him to life and thereby reinstated him as the heir who would carry on the family name.

Through this act of compassionate power, Jesus restored to life not only *one* person but *two*. For all practical purposes, the mother had died along with her son. As a widow, she was left with no one to defend her honor, her rights and the security of her household. Whereas the son had suffered a physical death, his mother was left to experience a socio-political death. Jesus' action saved them both.

Those who witnessed this remarkable event recognized that Jesus acted with power from God. The fear which seized them (v. 16) should be understood as that awe which springs from the realization of a divine action. Jesus was proclaimed as a prophet for his deeds which were similar to, albeit greater than, those of Elijah (1 Kings 17:8-24) and Elisha (2 Kings 4:18-36).

In Jesus, the people understood that God had *visited* his people (v. 16). A term which denoted both blessing and deliverance (Exodus 4:31, Ruth 1:6; Psalms 80:14, 106:4), the *visitation* of God in Jesus enabled all peoples, without distinction and despite the barriers which were thought to separate certain people from God (outcasts, poor, sinners, gentiles, etc.), to draw near. Later it would come to be known that God had not simply *visited* his people in Jesus; indeed, he had become *incarnate* in order to *live forever* in their midst.

*U*ntil God visited his people in Jesus, death was regarded as a barrier which forever separated the living from the dead. Because of Jesus, death is now recognized as a liberating passage to fuller life.

Be on guard!

When Pope Paul VI announced that he planned to visit Uganda in July of 1969, a flurry of preparations quickly began. Roadways on which the pope would travel were paved. Billboards were erected; one read, "Pepsi welcomes Pope Paul VI." Church and school choirs learned skits, songs and dances and practiced for hours to perfect their presentations. The shrine of the Uganda martyrs at Namugongo was refurbished and decorated.

All along the papal route, newly cut banana trees and colorful fresh flowers lined both sides of the road. Amid the flowers stood thousands of happy people, dressed in their best attire, singing and waving their welcome. Months of preparation and eager expectation were fulfilled in that moment when Uganda received the first pope to visit the country.

In the two short parables which comprise this reading from the Lucan gospel, preparedness for a distinguished visitor is also the featured lesson.

Biblical scholars agree that the call to watchfulness and readiness should be understood as applicable at each developmental stage of the gospel. For example, at its basic level of meaning, during the ministry of Jesus, the parables challenged Jesus' contemporaries to recognize that the Day of the Lord (Isaiah 13:6, Ezekiel 30:3, Amos 5:18, Joel 1:15 and 2:1) for which they had been eagerly waiting had indeed arrived *in him.*

By the time the evangelist wrote his gospel in the 80s CE, the parables served to alert Jesus' disciples to live in readiness for his return at the time of the parousia. Today, believers are called to heed the parables as a call to live in a state of watchfulness so as to be ready to meet Jesus (1) at his second coming and/or (2) in the individual encounter with him which comes at death.

In the first parable (vv. 35-38), the disciples of Jesus are instructed to fasten their belts and trim their lamps. The long,

flowing robes of the ancient Near Easterners were not condu-
cive to strenuous activity. Those who engaged in manual labor
had to tuck their robes in at the waist for better mobility.
Perhaps the disciples of Jesus were (and are) also meant to
recall that similar preparations were enjoined upon Israel at
the time of the exodus (Exodus 12:11, 22-23). Just as Israel
was to live in readiness for their encounter with freedom and
the passage to life, so are the disciples of Jesus to live in
watchfulness for their daily encounters with the Lord and
their eventual passage to fuller life.

The verbs which command such readiness are in the perfect imperative and present imperative tenses. This indicated
the need for a *constant* state of alertness. Last minute, hur-
ried preparations will not suffice. In other words, an interim
ethic, however valiant and extreme, is not a valid substitute
for a sure and steady, daily routine of readiness.

While the disciples in the first parable (vv. 35-38) could
be certain that the master *would return* but were unaware of
the *time* of his arrival, the head of the house in the second
parable (vv. 39-40) knew neither the time nor the mode of this
thief's appearance. The comparison of the coming of the Son of
Man to that of a thief is admittedly shocking but nevertheless
effective.

*For believers, the message is clear. Just as nostalgic memories
of bygone days when front doors could be left unlocked and
possessions unguarded have yielded to an era of security sys-
tems, neighborhood watch groups and self-defense courses, so
those who wait for Jesus must be no less thorough and realistic
in their preparations.*

*Like the disciples who were gifted with an absolutely unheard
of reward (the master put on an apron and served them at
table!), so the watchful and faithful believers in Jesus are to be
blessed with a share in the eucharistic feast in this life and a
place at the eschatological banquet in the next.*

The Jesus factor

*T*hree men were executed at Skull Place that day. By all appearances, they were three criminals whose deeds and their consequences had finally collided; Roman justice had prevailed. But Luke, in his telling of this event, supplies details which cause his readers to think and which afford the believer further insight into the meaning of that moment. The man in the middle made all the difference.

When Martin Dibelius (1883-1947), the German Lutheran biblical scholar, described the difference in the actions and attitudes of Jesus' disciples *before* and *after* his death and resurrection, he attributed those differences to what he called the X-factor. It was this X-factor (or, more correctly, the *Jesus* factor) which made a profound difference in the lives of his disciples and would consequently make a difference in the life of every believer. This difference has been dramatically illustrated in this uniquely Lucan portrayal of Jesus on the cross.

In death as in life, Jesus was in the midst of transgressors. The evangelist accented this fact throughout Jesus' ministry by describing his predilection for sinners and outcasts, On the cross, hanging between two criminals (in Greek, *kakourgoi*), Jesus' situation recalled that of the suffering servant who was described in this way: "Because he surrendered himself to death and was counted among the wicked, he shall take away the sins of the many and win pardon for their offenses" (Isaiah 53:12). In life and in death, the innocent Jesus was the factor that made a difference in the lives of sinners.

In contrast to the blasphemy of one of the criminals, the other acknowledged his guilt and the deserved punishment. Proclaiming Jesus' innocence ("This man has done nothing wrong"), he then called Jesus by name and made the request ("Jesus, remember me when you enter upon your reign") that was actually a confession of faith in Jesus' power to save. For this reason, Robert J. Karris has called this short pericope "the gospel within the gospel." Contained herein is the *crux* (!)

of Lucan theology: On the *cross* and through his death, Jesus has made the difference between life and death for all of humankind. In his second volume, Luke restated his soteriology in the speech of Peter before the Sanhedrin: "There is no salvation through anyone else, nor is there any other name under heaven given to the human race by which we are to be saved" (Acts 4:12).

Earlier in the gospel, the climax of Jesus' saving mission on the cross had been described in terms of the *"exodus"* that he would accomplish in Jerusalem (Luke 9:31). Jesus had also promised that he had the power to confer the *kingdom* upon his disciples (Luke 22:29-30). According to the plan of the Father, as revealed through the Hebrew scriptures (see Luke 24:26), Jesus had come to his exodus on the cross. Because of his exodus or passage from death to life, he could open the forgiveness and healing of the kingdom not only to the penitent criminal but to all. "This day you will be with me in paradise" affirms the saving power of Jesus and underscores the difference he can make in the lives of those who turn to him.

Three terms emphasize the importance of the Jesus factor. (1) *This day* does not indicate a specific day on the calendar; rather, it refers to the Day of the Lord or the era of messianic salvation which had become a here-and-now reality in the saving death of Jesus. (2) *Paradise* is derived from an ancient Persian word (*pairidaêza*) for an enclosed or walled garden. Persian kings paid special honor to certain of their subjects by inviting them to walk with them in their garden. After considerable adaptation, the term appeared in the intertestamental literature (Testament of Levi 18:10-11; 1 Enoch 17-19, 60:8) where it referred to the place of the righteous after death. (3) *With me* (i.e., to be with Jesus) is really the essence of paradise; as Ambrose commented, "Life is to be with Christ because, where Christ is, there is the kingdom."

Each of us will die one day. Each of us will experience the passage and the encounter with Christ that brings both truth and judgment. If Jesus has been a key factor throughout our struggle with living, he shall also be a factor in our dying. He alone makes all the difference.

He has been raised!

"Why do you search for the living one among the dead?" With this question, those who came to Jesus' tomb that day— as well as those who continue to read the account of those events—are invited to embrace in faith the significance of Jesus' death and resurrection. Jesus is not dead; he is not a tragic figure, relegated to the past by a cruel and untimely death. He is alive and remains a powerful, personal reality whose presence never ceases to challenge, guide, console and strengthen the believer.

Bowed to the ground, the terrified witnesses at the tomb that day were directed to change their perspective. They were sent forth from that moment to find and to experience the living one in the exigencies and joys and sorrows of their everyday lives. Later, in his testimony to the Christ-event, the Lucan author would again use a question to spur a change in perspective and as a catalyst to spawn the mission of the church. When the disciples lingered at the Mount of Olives, gazing into the clouds after Jesus' return to the Father, they were asked, "Why are you standing there looking at the sky?" (Acts 1:11). The reality of Jesus, alive and ever present, summoned them to service. They were to make known to all peoples the meaning of his words and works and the power of his resurrection.

The profound implications of Jesus' saving death and resurrection for believers have been further elucidated by other details in this Lucan narrative. Darkness at midday was a frightening phenomenon which recalled the ancient prophecies concerning the Day of the Lord. Promised by God as a time of judgment against the wickedness and infidelity of his people (Zephaniah 1:15, Amos 8:9, Joel 3:3-4), the Day of the Lord with its indictment of evil was truly realized on the day of Jesus' dying.

Another aspect of Jesus' saving death is underscored by the tearing of the temple curtain. During his ministry, Jesus continually challenged those religious and social structures which distinguished the righteous from the sinner, the clean from the unclean, the holy from the defiled. These distinctions and their implicit judgments served not only to categorize people; they also separated people from one another and from God. This separation extended to and was epitomized by the temple curtain which restricted the people from entering the Holy of Holies, the special site of God's presence. With the tearing of the sanctuary curtain, all such criteria for separation were declared obsolete; Jesus' death enabled all to enjoy free, unencumbered access to God (see also Hebrews 9:3, 9:8, 10:19ff; Ephesians 2:14-16).

Besides the cosmic response of creation (darkness) and that of the Jewish temple, others present at Jesus' death bore witness to its transforming effect. Moved to faith by the events of that day, the centurion (who was probably the officer in charge of the crucifixion) pronounced Jesus innocent and gave glory to God.

Throughout his passion account, Luke had insisted upon Jesus' innocence (Luke 23:4, 14-15, 22, 41). These repeated assertions, as well as the words of Jesus' own prayer ("Father, into your hands I commend my spirit"), served to portray Jesus as the suffering, faithful, innocent one who would be delivered by God (Isaiah 52:13—53:12, Wisdom 2:18, Psalm 31). Whereas the other synoptic evangelists (Mark 15:39, Matthew 27:54) have the centurion declaring Jesus as the Son of God, the Lucan version accents his *innocence.*

As Charles Talbert has noted, for Matthew and Mark, the centurion is a christologist; for Luke, he is an apologist. The mention of the centurion's glorifying God reprised a recurring theme in the Lucan gospel. Those who witnessed a revelation of God's power and mercy in the words and works of Jesus typically responded with praise or glory for God (Luke 2:20, 5:25-26, 7:16, 13:13, 17:15, 18:43).

Additional testimony to the redeeming power of Jesus' death can be seen in the attitude of the crowd. No doubt, many had come to the place called the Skull out of curiosity, attracted by what they had heard of Jesus and the furor his presence had caused. The events of that day effected a change in those who had gathered; curiosity yielded to compunction. The action of beating the breast was associated with guilt and contrition as well as with mourning. Through this action, the salvific effect of Jesus' suffering is evidenced in the lives of those for whom he died.

At death, each of us will find Jesus in a special way. Our search for him, the living one, is a quest which must occupy our minds and involve our energies here and now. Through this daily search, the process of our redemption and transformation is begun. Through this daily searching, we bear witness to his saving power and we glorify God.

Stay with us!

When a loved one dies, those who are left behind become engaged, consciously or not, in a process of healing. Seeking solace and support in a variety of ways, some turn to friends and relatives; there is much talking, sharing, praying, crying and even laughter. Others, in a more solitary manner, grieve their loss by sifting through photographs, by rereading old letters and cards, by visiting the gravesite, by touching and smelling the things that belonged to the one who has died.

At times, the belongings of the deceased are left as they were. I once heard of a widow who saved an arrangement of balloons given to her by her husband for their anniversary because he had blown them up and, as such, they still contained a part of him she could not bear to lose. Whatever the course an individual's grieving may take, the character of the process is usually similar: Remembering the loved one creates a sort of presence and sustains a bond that eventually brings about healing.

The two disciples of Jesus who were travelling from Jerusalem to Emmaus were grieving, and their sadness was tinged with disappointment. Besides losing Jesus, they had also lost the hope they shared for the political and religious future of Israel. In this wonderful resurrection appearance narrative, the Lucan evangelist makes it clear that Jesus had certainly not been lost to his people, nor was the hope they had placed in him to remain unfulfilled. Jesus did not leave behind photographs or letters, but he did bless believers with the legacy of his abiding presence.

That the risen Jesus was somehow transformed is evidenced by the fact that the two travelers did not recognize him. Nevertheless, like the other evangelists, Luke was careful to establish the continuity between the risen Lord and the earthly Jesus. To that end, he portrayed Jesus ministering to his own as he had done before his death: He taught them, interpreted Moses and the prophets and opened their eyes to the truth. For the disciples, however, full recognition of Jesus came only at the evening meal.

At that point on their journey, when it seemed as if Jesus was about to take his leave, the disciples invited him, "Stay with us." In the words and actions that followed, Jesus revealed the manner in which he would indeed stay with us and forever be present to his own. Just as he had done at so many meals before, "he took bread, blessed it, broke it and gave it to them" (Luke 9:11-17, 22:19-20).

The table fellowship they had known before Jesus' death was now resumed by the risen Lord. In that moment, their eyes were opened. "Opened eyes" is a frequent Lucan theme, (occurring six times in Luke-Acts); it signified a deeper understanding of an event or of a revelation.

The fact that Jesus vanished at this point did not dampen their joy or lessen their eagerness to share their experience of his presence. The disciples had learned that the risen Lord Jesus would continue to be present in the breaking of the bread. Their contact with him would not be lost; rather, through their eucharistic sharing, they would know the healing and new life which had been given to them through the breaking of his body on the cross. A day that began with grieving had evolved into healing and joy.

By the time Luke wrote Luke-Acts in the 80s CE, believers had become accustomed to experiencing and celebrating Jesus' continued presence among them in the breaking of the bread (Acts 2:46). Today, at each eucharistic celebration, the Emmaus encounter with Jesus is renewed. During the liturgy of the word, the faithful are nourished with the bread of the living word (Luke 24:27). With the sharing of the eucharistic bread (and wine), all are fed and healed with the presence of the living Lord.

Life, present and future

"*H*e's making a list, checking it twice, gonna find out who's naughty or nice. . . . He sees you when you're sleeping, he knows when you're awake. . . . He knows if you've been bad or good, so be good, for goodness' sake!" The words of this song, popular at Christmas particularly among children, attribute an uncanny ability to Santa Claus, viz., to know and to judge the activities of every child in the world and to respond to their Christmas wish lists accordingly. A pleasant myth that each of us eventually outgrows, this notion of Santa Claus has tempered the behavior of many a small child eager for Christmas goodies.

For some people, maturation to adulthood involves an all too simplistic reworking of this myth in regard to God. The jolly roly-poly Christmas figure is replaced by the divine judge; and human behavior all through life is regulated in such a way as to be found worthy of God's approval and rewards at death. But this reading from the fourth gospel summons believers to reconsider their notion of the last things and to permit this consideration to affect present existence in a profound manner. Eternal life is so much more than a reward for good behavior; it is the gratuitous gift of *knowing* the Lord as he reveals himself today, tomorrow and forever.

Two "Amen, amen" statements (vv. 24, 25) introduce the pericope, indicating the gravity of the information for the life of the believer. Both statements reflect the Johannine gospel's unique perspective on eschatology. More than an event of the future which will occur at the end of a person's earthly life (bringing with it judgment, and reward or punishment), eschatology is also a present consideration.

It is significant that the Johannine Jesus promises, "Whoever *hears* my word and *believes* . . . *has* eternal life . . . *has passed* from death to life" (v. 24). The present tense of the verbs underscores the notion of *realized* eschatology. Rather than envision the passage from death to life as a journey which begins *only* at death, the fourth gospel sees this passage as a journey which is made in increments—day by day, word by word, deed by deed, thought by thought.

The realized eschatology presented in the fourth gospel hinges upon its distinctive christology. In Jesus, who is the word of God spoken into human flesh in the realm of time and space, God reveals himself in a definitive way. That revelation of God in Jesus creates a situation of crisis (the root of which means "judgment" in Greek). Jesus' presence in the world provokes a self-judgment on the part of those who hear what he says and see what he does. Those who choose Jesus and allow that fundamental option to determine every other aspect of their existence choose life; those who reject Jesus thereby judge themselves by that very fact and choose death.

To balance this view of realized eschatology, the remainder of this text alludes to the *future* or final eschatology (vv. 26-29) at which time the Son of Man will exercise his role as judge. Functioning as the apocalyptic Son of Man of Daniel 7:13, the Son of Man will oversee the resurrection of both the good and the evil. On the basis of their faith and the authenticity of that faith reflected in deeds, judgment will be rendered: The good shall receive life and the evil shall know condemnation (see Daniel 12:2).

Jesus' claim to act as both judge and lifegiver should be viewed within the literary context of the gospel. Immediately before this discourse, Jesus had cured a man on the Sabbath (John 5:1-18). Angry at this breach of the holy day, the Jews berated Jesus who argued that he was doing his Father's work. Such a claim was tantamount to claiming equality with God. In the discourse that follows (vv. 19-30), Jesus is presented as claiming as his own the divine prerogatives of giving life and of judging. The rabbis taught that, even during the Sabbath's prescribed rest, God exercised that double prerogative (Tal. Bab. Taanith 2a). Jesus' works performed on the Sabbath enunciated his true identity. His words underscore the importance of a personal and present faith as the only viable preparation for a future and final encounter with him.

For the believer, death's final passage has already begun. Each time Jesus' word is heard and kept in faith, each time a decision is made for Jesus and because of him, the believer has eternal life. When the passage from death to life is complete, the believer shall rise to live forever in Jesus.

Who sees me. . . .

An equestrian statue of Rodrigo Díaz de Vivar (1043-1099), also known as El Cid (from the Arabic *sidi*, "leader" or "lord"), stands in front of the bridge of San Pablo in Burgos, Spain. A medieval military leader and national hero, El Cid and his conquests have been memorialized in epic poems, plays and films. Because of his powerful presence, he was feared by his enemies and revered by those in his command.

Although legend has played an active role in the telling of his exploits, certain details of his life are widely attested. For example, during one particularly violent siege, his men (who were greatly outnumbered by their adversaries) began to urge him to retreat to safer ground. Ignoring their pleas, El Cid mounted his horse, Babieca, and charged to the forefront of his troops. When they saw him, they forgot their fear and fought to victory. Even after El Cid had died in battle, his lifeless body was secured upright upon his horse. Those who looked on him were bolstered by that vision and fought their way back from defeat.

For ten years after his death, the embalmed body of El Cid remained seated on an ivory chair in the monastery of San Pedro de Cardeña. Even in death, his presence had the power to move all who came to see him. Like El Cid, the Johannine Jesus appeals to his disciples to *look* upon him, to *see* him and to be moved, not to battle but to that faith which brings eternal life (v. 40).

In his gospel, the fourth evangelist employed a series of five verbs which expressed the idea of looking or seeing. In this particular pericope, the verb used is the Greek *theorein*. As Raymond E. Brown has explained, "*Theorein* means to look at with concentration." It implies a look that lingers, studies carefully, considers slowly. As it appears in this text, *theorein* (v. 40) means to truly perceive and accept Jesus in faith.

Precisely what were the disciples to perceive and believe of Jesus? As the remaining verses of the text point out, Jesus was to be seen and accepted as one who had come down from heaven to do the will of the Father (v. 38). The will of the Father was to give over to Jesus all who would come to him (v. 37) so that none would be lost (v. 39) and that all would be raised up on the last day (v. 40).

At this point, 20th-century believers may be inclined to ask how they could possibly *look upon* or *see* Jesus. Some may even envy Jesus' first-century contemporaries who had the privilege of seeing what he did and how he lived. But, as the gospels indicate in numerous instances, many who *saw* the wonders Jesus did still did *not* believe in him or accept him. Physical sight evolved to spiritual insight only through the act of *choosing to believe* in Jesus. Seeing *and* believing led to eternal life.

It must be noted that this text is excerpted from the lengthy bread of life discourse in John 6. Within the context of the discourse, these verses follow immediately upon Jesus' declaration, "I am the bread of life; whoever comes to me will never hunger and whoever believes in me will never thirst" (John 6:35). Throughout the discourse, the term "bread of life" is used in both a sapiential and sacramental sense. In other words, "bread of life" referred to the revelation of God in and by Jesus as well as the living bread of his body, sacrificially broken on the cross and eucharistically shared at the last supper for the life of the world. With this in mind, Jesus' invitation to see him and to believe takes on added significance.

Each time the good news of salvation is proclaimed, believers have the opportunity to see *Jesus and* believe. *At each eucharistic celebration, Jesus' living presence can be* seen *and accepted in faith. In the eyes of the poor, homeless, hungry, sick and imprisoned with whom he identified, Jesus can be* seen. *Those who* see *him and are moved to faith at his powerful presence will have eternal life.*

Food for eternal life

*I*n March 1513, Spanish navigator Juan Ponce de León set sail from Puerto Rico, bound for the Bahamas. He had learned from the natives about a certain island called Bimini, on which there was thought to exist a marvelous spring that could rejuvenate those who drank from it. Although he eventually found Bimini and later became the military governor of the island, the explorer never located the mythical fountain of youth.

Not unique in his quest, Ponce de León is one of many throughout history whose desire for never-ending life led to great adventure and unusual feats. The ancient Romans and Egyptians drank pearls dissolved in vinegar, believing that this extravagance could prolong life. Thousands of herbal remedies, elixirs, tonics and potions have been invented in an effort to cheat death. Even today, the obsession with living longer is reflected in the virtual mountain of literature written on the subject.

When Jesus spoke of eternal life to the crowds that followed him to Capernaum that day (John 6:24), they were probably intrigued by his words. And when he said that he could give them the food that endures for eternal life (John 6:27), they clamored in excitement to receive it. But when he identified *himself* as that food, many found his words too hard to accept. They did not believe; they turned away (John 6:60, 64, 66).

This pericope is part of the lengthy bread of life discourse which followed the sign of the multiplication of the loaves (John 6:1-15) and within which the Johannine evangelist gathered all the eucharistic material of his gospel. Set within the context of the Jewish feast of Passover, John 6 could be regarded as a new and Christian understanding of Passover. Because of Jesus' saving death, those who believe in him pass over from slavery to freedom, from death to life. In this particular part of the discourse, the statement in v. 51, "The

211

bread I will give is my flesh for the life of the world," describes the sacrificial and saving death of Jesus on the cross. The following verses elucidate the way in which believers may appropriate and share in the salvation wrought by Jesus, viz., by eating the bread and drinking the wine which he has identified as his flesh and blood.

Raymond E. Brown explains that, in order to have any positive meaning whatsoever, the terms "flesh" and "blood" must refer to the eucharist. "To eat the flesh of another" was a Semitism for slanderous, hostile action (Psalm 27:2). The drinking of blood was absolutely repugnant to Jews, forbidden by law (Genesis 9:4, Leviticus 3:17) and equivalent to brutal slaughter (Jeremiah 46:10). Flesh and blood, in this pericope, should be understood as they were in the Hebrew scriptures, i.e., as a designation for the life of a living person.

In the flesh and blood of Jesus, i.e., in his very life, believers have union with him and the experience of eternal life. Note the *present* tense (and implied realized eschatology) of the verbs in this pericope: "if anyone *eats*," "he who *feeds*," "*remains* in me and I in him." But there is also a sense of the *future* as well: "*shall live* forever," "I *will raise* him up on the last day," "*will have* life because of me."

In the bread of life, every aspect and dimension of human hope is realized. The past *saving event of the cross is remembered and celebrated. Those who share the bread of life in the* present *receive therein a taste and a promise of all the goodness which is yet to come in the* future. *Like no other food and like no other gift, the bread of life which is the eucharist blesses those who believe with life—now and for eternity.*

Yes, Lord, I believe!

*T*o coin a well-known phrase, Lazarus was "the straw that broke the camel's back." Throughout his public ministry, the Johannine Jesus' teaching and activities brought him into conflict with the recognized religious authorities of his day. He healed on the Sabbath and explained that he was doing the work of his Father in heaven. Accused of blasphemy and of claiming equality with God, Jesus also caused a stir when he spoke of the demise of the temple. He called himself the light of the world and the source of living water. Jesus associated with Samaritans and declared that those who kept his word would never die.

Within the fourth gospel, the controversial teachings and activities of Jesus are presented as signs. In each of the seven signs of the fourth gospel, some aspect of Jesus' person and mission was revealed; those who witnessed the signs were challenged to believe. Some turned to him in faith, others saw him as a threat and turned away in disbelief. Ironically, it was the last and greatest of the seven signs which set into motion the plot that would end Jesus' life. The proverbial "straw that broke the camel's back" was the raising to life of Lazarus. Through this event, Jesus is revealed as the resurrection and the life, and as the messiah, the Son of God (John 11:25, 27).

While arguing Jesus' fate, Caiphas spoke the words that perfectly summed up the character and purpose of his ministry: "that one man would die for the people" (John 11:50). Fraught with Johannine irony, the statement underscored the belief of the early church, viz., Jesus the Lord of life had come to die so that "whoever believes in him, even if he die, will live" and so that "everyone who lives and believes in him will never die" (John 11:25-26).

According to this narrative, Martha professed the belief, shared by many of the Jews of the first century CE, that there would be a resurrection of the dead on the last day (John 11:24). This doctrine, disputed by the Sadducees, was incorporated into Israelite theology in the early second century BCE (see Daniel 12:2). Throughout the Lazarus event, the Johannine Jesus invited Martha (and all who believe) to understand that resurrected life was not simply a *future* blessing but also a gift for the *present*. As Raymond E. Brown has explained, "In Johannine realized eschatology, the gift of life that conquers death is a present reality in Jesus Christ (John 11:25-26)."

During the course of this lengthy narrative (John 11:1-44), Lazarus is identified as Jesus' "friend" and as "the one Jesus loves." These references point not only to Jesus' motivation for raising Lazarus but also to the raison d'être of his earthly mission; that motivation is love. Just as the love of the Father was the impetus for Jesus' coming into the world (John 3:16), so the love of Jesus was the impetus for the gift of his own life for the life of the world (John 15:13). Love is also to be the motivation for keeping Jesus' word and his commandments (John 14:23, 15) as well as the sign of discipleship (John 15:12).

In addition to being the recipient of Jesus' special love, Lazarus can be understood as the paradigm of the Christian believer. Like Lazarus who was called from death and restored to life by Jesus, every believer is called from the death of sin and alienation to the new life of forgiveness and reconciliation. Jesus extends this call from death to life each day of our earthly existence. Each time we respond to his call in faith and love, we realize the mystery of his Passover in our lives. When the time of our final passage arrives, we shall know the power of his resurrection forever.

Life

That Jesus had the power to *give life* and that he was (and is) indeed the *source of life* is a recurrent theme in the fourth gospel. From the very first words of the prologue wherein Jesus is proclaimed as the word who is both the life and the light of the human race (John 1:3) to the conclusion of the gospel which promises *life* to those who believe in him as the messiah, Son of God (John 20:31), the equation is constantly and clearly reiterated: Jesus is life!

In the episode with Nicodemus, Jesus is portrayed as the gift of a loving Father for the *life* and salvation of the world (John 3:16). To the Samaritan woman at Jacob's well, Jesus was revealed as the source of *life-giving* water (John 4:14). In the sign of the loaves and through the ensuing discourse at Capernaum, Jesus made himself known as the bread of *life* (John 6). At the feast of Tabernacles, he invited believers to find in him the light of *life* which dispels the darkness (John 8:12). In the cures of the official's son and the crippled man at the pool of Bethesda, Jesus is portrayed as one who could speak a *life-giving* word. The discourse which follows these healing events underscored the power of the Son to give *life* to whomever he chooses (John 5:11-29).

Inextricably bound to the many attestations of Jesus as the life of the world is the reality that his gift of life to others would involve Jesus' own death. Declaring that he would be "lifted up [i.e., on the cross] so that everyone who believes in him may have eternal life" (John 3:14-15) and that he is the good shepherd who would freely and of his own volition lay down his life for his sheep (Jesus 10:15-18), Jesus linked his own passage from death to life with that of everyone who believes in him.

In the raising to life of Lazarus, which is the last and greatest sign of the fourth gospel, all the many references to the life-giving power of Jesus' words and works have been drawn together in a dramatic climax. Ironically, while this event served to definitively identify Jesus as the resurrection and the life, it also precipitated the sounding of his death knell in the Sanhedrin (John 11:25, 50-51).

The dual reference to Jesus' being troubled in spirit (vv. 33, 38) has been a source of consternation among scholars who have proposed a variety of motivation for Jesus' feelings. Some have suggested that the term *embrimasthai,* which implies the emotion of anger, indicated that Jesus was annoyed at the lack of faith of those who wept and mourned Lazarus' death. But Jesus *also* wept for his friend and, as the gospels attest in numerous instances, he was extraordinarily *patient* with the insufficient faith of his contemporaries. More conceivable is the suggestion of John Chrysostom that Jesus was so moved by the death of his friend because of the implied presence of Satan and of the kingdom of evil with which Jesus was continually in conflict. With an authoritative shout for his friend to come out of his tomb, Jesus' power to give life, not only to Lazarus but to all who believe, is illustrated. Fulfilled also in this action is the promise Jesus made earlier in the gospel, viz., "the hour is coming in which all who are in the tombs will hear his voice and come out, those who have done good deeds to the resurrection of life, but those who have done wicked deeds to the resurrection of condemnation" (John 5:28-29).

One final lesson in this wonderful episode is the fact that Jesus prayed when confronted by the somber passage which is death. As Pheme Perkins has noted, "Gestures of prayer on Jesus' part are always expressions of the relationship between Jesus and the Father." It is these very gestures and that same relationship which will sustain each believer when his/her moment of passage arrives.

Like a seed

Each spring, the earth experiences a renewal. Birds that journeyed elsewhere for the winter return. Barren trees remember their leaves. Grass that turned brown under the snow grows green once again. Mail boxes are filled with seed catalogues whose colorful promises of flowers and vegetables invite farmers and gardeners to enter into that wondrous process which begins in seeming death and ends with abundant, vibrant harvest. Anyone who has ever planted a seed and waited for it to grow has experienced something of the mystery to which Jesus summoned his disciples in this pericope.

The season was Passover and his contemporaries were celebrating the annual remembrance of their liberation from slavery and the renewal of their covenantal relationship with Yahweh. In the midst of those festivities, Jesus invited those who would put their faith in him to understand this liberation and their relationship to God in a new and fuller way.

By the announcement that the "hour has come" (v. 23), the Johannine author drew to a climax some 26 references in his gospel concerning Jesus' hour. Most of these references did not refer to time in a chronological sense (in Greek, *chronos*) but rather to that special moment (in Greek, *kairos*) or hour for which Jesus had come among us, viz., the event when Jesus returned to his Father. This new Passover event—to be accomplished through Jesus' passion, death, resurrection and ascension—would thereby effect the liberation or salvation of all peoples from sin and death and forge a new and eternal relationship with the Father.

While Jesus equated the *hour* of his passage from death to life with *glory* (vv. 23, 27-28), he also acknowledged the reality of the suffering which he was willing to accept. The imminence of his hour filled Jesus with ambivalence. Troubled in spirit (v. 27), he was nevertheless resolute in his desire to do the will of his Father.

Although the fourth evangelist did not include a Gethsemane episode in his account of Jesus' passion, this text contains all the elements mentioned by the synoptic authors, viz., the acknowledgment that his hour had come, the anguish, the prayerful appeal to the Father, the willing acceptance of the ordeal and the consoling affirmation from above. The voice from the sky (v. 28) is reminiscent of the voice which approved and acclaimed Jesus at his baptism and transfiguration (see synoptic accounts). But as Raymond E. Brown has suggested, the closest parallel is to be found in the pseudepigraphical Testament of Levi which stated: "The skies shall be opened and sanctification shall come upon him from the temple of glory with the Father's voice, as from Abraham to Isaac; and the glory of the most high shall be uttered over him" (Testament of Levi 18:6-7). This late apocalyptic writing, also known to the community at Qumran, was replete with references to "God appearing in the flesh to deliver his people" and to the coming messiah as the "savior of the world." The voice from heaven underscored the belief that his people's hopes for divine intervention and salvation would be fulfilled in Jesus and through the hour of his passage to glory.

Finally, this passage also contains an instruction (vv. 24-26) for all who would become the beneficiaries of Jesus' hour. To appropriate the gift of his passage, believers must "lose" their lives in service and in self-giving so as to preserve them for eternal life. The "losing" or "hating" of one's life implies a willingness to participate *personally* and *really* in Jesus' death—to die as the grain of wheat dies, so as to produce life and fruit. "Fruit" could be understood in association with John 4:36, where the *fruit* of the harvest referred to the *people* who were, in faith, coming to Jesus and in him to the Father.

Those who believe in the Son of Man are called to live *in such as way as to bring others to him and to* die *in the firm hope that his hour has assured us of life eternal.*

Have faith

*T*hat the birds of worry and care fly above your head, this you cannot change. But that they build nests in your hair, this you can prevent!

This ancient Chinese proverb conjures up an amusing verbal image whose point is clear. The average human life is filled with opportunities for worry. It is the wise person who does not allow anxiety to sap his joy and vitality. But whereas the Chinese proverb ascribed to a method of contemplation and rational self-control in order to ward off fear and its consequences, Jesus called his disciples to exercise another human capacity: faith. "Faith in God, faith in Jesus" (John 14:1) is the antidote for troubled hearts.

According to the Johannine author, faith is to be understood as a knowing acceptance of and active commitment to Jesus (or God). Not a purely emotional or affective commitment, true faith also includes a willingness to accede to God's demands (1 John 3:23) as they are presented in and by Jesus.

Jesus' imminent departure was a source of anxiety for his followers. While he was with them, his presence centered and strengthened them, but the thought of his absence filled them with dread.

In this short pericope, the Johannine Jesus offers his disciples the assurance that their impending separation would not sever their ties with him. On the contrary, Jesus' journey home to the Father, soon to be accomplished through the "hour" of his passion, death and glorification, would also effect the passage home of all who believe.

William Barclay has explained that Jesus' promise to "go and prepare a place" means that he will act as our *prodromos* ("forerunner" in Greek, see Hebrews 6:20). In ancient times, *prodromoi* (plural) referred to the special reconnaissance troops who were sent out ahead to blaze the trail and secure a safe path for the rest of the army. The same term referred to the small pilot boat sent ahead of the great merchant ships to secure a safe passage into a dangerous or difficult harbor. As our *prodromos,* Jesus has blazed the passage and secured the way from death to life for believers.

An additional source of comfort and a deterrent to anxiety is the promise of "many dwelling places" in the Father's house. Variously interpreted, the *mone* ("dwelling places") were represented in Jewish apocalyptic literature as the eternal habitations of those who had died, the quality of those accommodations being determined by the person's conduct on earth: "In the world to come, there are many mansions prepared for men—good for good, evil for evil" (Slavonic Enoch 41:2). This notion of the varying degrees of heaven's rest and rewards also found its way into the writings of the early fathers of the church (Irenaeus, Clement of Alexandria). Today, scholars understand the reference to *many* dwelling places to mean simply that there will be room for *all* in the Father's house.

Traditionally understood to mean heaven, the term "my Father's house" (in conjunction with the "many dwelling places") takes on deeper significance. The same term, occurring in John 2:16, referred to the Jerusalem *temple* but was later applied to Jesus' *body* (John 2:19-22). Another reference in John 8:35 compares the privilege of a *son* to that of a *slave*; the son will always have a (dwelling) place in the home of his father. This special house ("my Father's house") "where the son has a permanent dwelling place suggests a *union* with the Father reserved for Jesus the Son, and for all those who are begotten as God's children by the Spirit Jesus gives" (Raymond E. Brown). Thus, the "many dwelling places in my Father's house" could be understood as an eternal participation in the union which Jesus shares with the Father.

Still fearful because of Jesus' leaving, Thomas (who functions as the fourth gospel's representative of doubt and skepticism) queries Jesus with regard to the *way* to the Father's house. In a statement which sums up Johannine soteriology, Jesus himself is declared to be the way, the truth and the life. As both the mediator of God's saving love and the exemplar of the perfect human response to that love, Jesus is truly the way.

*O*ne day, each of us will face the worrisome and fearful reality of death. Jesus, who is the source of life and truth, is also our way to the Father's house. He is our brother and forerunner; his passage has assured our own.

Gifts of love and glory

Anyone who has been in attendance at the deathbed of another will probably never forget the experience. In the last moments of human existence, words and gestures take on a deeper significance. What is witnessed and what is spoken are engraved on the minds and hearts of loved ones, to be recalled again and again as if to grasp one more time a moment of union with the one who has died.

In the funeral rituals (both secular and sacred) that surround human dying, the living linger together and comfort one another with shared memories. They cite the accomplishments of the deceased individual, remember qualities and idiosyncrasies, generously put aside faults and failures. In addition to these last shared moments, most of us will have prepared a will in which we relegate to those we leave behind the material possessions we have acquired.

But none of us, however great or important our life and its achievements, can ever bequeath to another the gift of our abiding presence. Only Jesus had the capacity to make such a testament, as revealed in this beautiful passage from John's gospel.

Part of a longer text (which has become known as Jesus' high priestly prayer), these particular verses are from that part of the prayer in which Jesus prayed for those who would come to believe in him through the witness of other disciples. Situated in the context of the lengthy last supper discourse and purported to be Jesus' final words of farewell, this text is fully informed with Johannine theology and christology.

Aware that his death is imminent, Jesus nevertheless prays that those given him by the Father will be *in his company, where he is.* He also asserts that he will *continue to* reveal the Father's name to his disciples.

As explained elsewhere in the gospel, Jesus' abiding presence and continuing revelation is due to the activity of the paraclete (John 14:26, 16:13). As Raymond E. Brown has fur-

ther explained, "This continued deepening of the understanding of the revelation of God in Jesus has as its purpose
and goal the indwelling of Jesus in the Christian (verse 26). If
the last two lines of verse 26 are compared, it will be noted
that the presence of Jesus in the Christian stands in parallelism with the presence of the love of God in the Christian."
These two realities—the abiding presence of Jesus and the indwelling love of God—were identified in later trinitarian theology as the gift of the Holy Spirit.

Jesus' prayer also expressed his intention that his glory
be seen and shared by those who believe in him. A gift of the
Father to Jesus, motivated by love (v. 24), the concept of glory
in the fourth gospel is solidly founded in the Hebrew scriptures. There, the glory of God is understood as a visible manifestation of God in an *act of power,* e.g., in the gift of manna
which sustained the people in the wilderness (Exodus 16:7-10)
or in the cloud and pillar of fire which assured Israel of the
divine presence (Exodus 16:10, 24:17).

. When Jesus became flesh, he became the incarnation or
embodiment of that glory in time and space (John 1:14). In his
words and works, the glory of God was revealed (John 2:11,
11:40, 17:4) and, through the hour of his passion on the cross
(which Jesus referred to, not as his suffering or even as his
death but as his *glorification*), Jesus made fully manifest the
presence and power of the Father (John 12:23, 28; 13:32; 17:1).

*By virtue of his saving hour, Jesus' legacy to his own is one of
glory, peace, presence and love. Those who live and believe in
him are always in his company. Those who make the passage
through death with him will always know his love.*

Victor, not victim

Although the 1967 Arab-Israeli war closed down the work of archaeologist Kathleen Kenyon in Jerusalem, it was not before she had succeeded in identifying the knoll called Golgotha, or Place of the Skull, where Jesus died. In the fourth century, Constantine had built the Church of the Holy Sepulcher on the site and, since that time, Christians have venerated it as holy place.

The subject of great controversy because it now stands *within* the city walls, recent excavations there have revealed that, in Jesus' time, the location of the city's defensive walls was such that the site known as Golgotha was indeed outside the walls of Jerusalem. More important, however, than its precise location are the events that transpired there during Passover season ca. 30 CE.

Jesus' hour had come. The time of his glorification (passion, death and resurrection) had arrived. While many Jews perceived him to be a blasphemer and a messianic pretender, while the Romans regarded him as a temporary threat to their judicial control of their province of Palestinium, believers look upon the dying Jesus as their source of life and salvation. It is from his posture as a *believer* that the fourth evangelist has portrayed Jesus in the hour of his death: not as a victim but as a victor.

Clearly showing Jesus "in charge" of the situation (with no mention of Simon of Cyrene as in the synoptics), John depicts him as "carrying the cross himself" (v. 17). A good son, Jesus carefully attended to the welfare of his mother. Only when he had completely fulfilled his mission did he signal the end and, of his own volition, hand over his spirit.

In addition to his presentation of Jesus as a willing sacrifice rather than a victim of political and/or religious controversy, the fourth evangelist has also supported his narrative with a series of scriptural references, all of which are fulfilled in Jesus' hour.

"I thirst" (v. 28) and the common wine offered Jesus (v. 29) recalled and fulfilled the words of the psalmists (Psalm 69:22, 22:16). Both of these psalms featured the prayer of a suffering, just person whose innocence God vindicates. Only the fourth gospel includes a reference to the sprig of hyssop (v. 29), the same plant used to smear the blood of the paschal lamb on the door posts and lintels of the Hebrews' homes in Egypt (Exodus 12:22). By this specific reference (and several others in the course of the passion), John depicts Jesus' death and its effects as a *new* Passover event. Jesus' statement, "It is finished" (v. 30), can be understood as his announcement that his "hour," which had begun in John 13:1, was now being consummated. Also implied in this statement is the fact that the work which the Father had entrusted to Jesus is now completed (John 8:29, 14:31, 16:32, 17:4). These words may also be reminiscent of the victory cry in Revelation 16:17 where a voice from the heavenly temple signals the end of the reign of evil.

By using the specific term *paradidonai* to describe Jesus' handing over his spirit, the evangelist recalled for his readers the suffering servant who similarly "*surrendered* himself to death and was counted among the wicked to take away the sins of many and win pardon for their offenses" (Isaiah 53:12).

Variously interpreted throughout the centuries, the scene with Mary and the beloved disciple is generally understood in terms of Mary as a new Eve (Genesis 3:15), mother of a new people (the church, represented by the beloved disciple) who are redeemed from death and brought to birth through the life-giving Spirit of Jesus. Mentioned only here and at the wedding celebration at Cana (John 2:3-5, 12), Mary appears in the fourth gospel as a model disciple whose faith in Jesus the early church emulated.

None of us knows the hour of our death, nor can we completely control the circumstances that will surround it. But, with firm faith and sure hope, we place our trust in Jesus whose saving, victorious hour has secured our passage and our peace.

Liturgical Index

This section lists separately the readings assigned to each of the three rites: baptism (infants), weddings and funerals.

Scriptural Index

This section lists together in their biblical sequence all of the readings for the three rules: baptism (infants), weddings and funerals. The boldface letters identify the ritual source of the reading: **B** = *baptism,* **W** = *weddings,* **F** = *funerals.*

First Reading

Genesis 1:26-28, 31 (**W**) *54*

Genesis 2:18-24 (**W**) *56*

Genesis 24:48-51, 58-67 (**M**) *58*

Exodus 17:3-7 (**B**) *2*

1 Kings 17:17-24 (**B**) *48*

2 Kings 4:8-37 (**B**) *50*

Tobit 7:9-10, 11-15 (**W**) *60*

Tobit 8:5-7 (**W**) *62*

2 Maccabees 12:43-46 (**F**) *137*

Job 19:1, 23-27 (**F**) *122*

Proverbs 31:10-13, 19-20, 30-31 (**W**) *70*

Song of Songs 2:8-10, 14, 15; 8:6-7 (**W**) *64*

Wisdom 3:1-9 (**F**) *125*

Wisdom 4:7-14 (**F**) *127*

Sirach 26:1-4, 13-16 (**W**) *66*

Isaiah 25:7-9 (**F**) *129*

Jeremiah 31:31-34 (**W**) *68*

Lamentations 3:17-26 (**F**) *131*

Ezekiel 36:24-28 (**B**) *4*

Ezekiel 47:1-9, 12 (**B**) *6*

Daniel 12:1-3 (**F**) *134*

Second Reading

Acts 10:34-43 (**F**) *140*

Romans 5:5-11 (**F**) *142*

Romans 5:17-21 (**F**) 145

Romans 6:3-5 (**B**) *8*

Romans 6:3-9 (**F**) *147*

Romans 8:14-23 (**F**) *149*

Romans 8:28-32 (**B**) *10*

Romans 8:31-35, 37-39 (**W**) *72,* (**F**) *152*

Romans 12:1-2, 9-19 (**W**) *74*

Romans 14:7-9, 10b-12 (**F**) *154*

Romans 15:1b-3a, 5-7, 13 (**W**) *76*

1 Corinthians 6:13-15, 17-20 (**W**) *78*

1 Corinthians 12:12-13 (**B**) *12*

1 Corinthians 12:31—13:8 (**W**) *80*

1 Corinthians 15:20, 23, 24, 28 (**F**) *156*

1 Corinthians 15:51-57 (**F**) *158*

2 Corinthians 4:14—5:1 (**F**) *160*

2 Corinthians 5:1, 6-10 (**F**) *162*